Copyright © 2006 by Sharina

• *Published and distributed in Australia by*: Hay House Australia Pty. Ltd.: www.hayhouse.com.au • *Published and distributed in the United States by*: Hay House, Inc.: www.hayhouse.com • *Published and distributed in the United Kingdom by*: Hay House UK, Ltd.: www.hayhouse.co.uk • *Published and distributed in the Republic of South Africa by*: Hay House SA (Pty), Ltd.: orders@psdprom.co.za • *Distributed in Canada by*: Raincoast: www.raincoast.com • *Published in India by*: Hay House Publications (India) Pvt. Ltd.: www.hayhouseindia.co.in

• *Edited by*: Serene Conneeley • *Designed by*: Rhett Nacson • *Illustrated by*: Dwayne Labbé
• *Cover Photo*: Charlie Surbey • *Author Photo*: Absolutely Glamorous

All rights reserved. No part of this book may be reproduced by any mechanical, photographic, or electronic process, or in the form of a phonographic recording; nor may it be stored in a retrieval system, transmitted, or otherwise be copied for public or private use—other than for "fair use" as brief quotations embodied in articles and reviews—without prior written permission of the publisher.

The author of this book does not dispense medical advice or prescribe the use of any technique as a form of treatment for physical, emotional, or medical problems without the advice of a physician, either directly or indirectly. The intent of the author is only to offer information of a general nature to help you in your quest for emotional and spiritual well-being. In the event you use any of the information in this book for yourself, which is your constitutional right, the author and the publisher assume no responsibility for your actions.

ISBN 13: 978-1-4019-1804-0
ISBN 10: 1-4019-1804-2

09 08 07   7 6 5 4 3 2
1st printing in Australia, August 2006
2nd printing in Australia, February 2007

Printed in Australia by Griffin Press

by Sharina

Hay House, Inc.
Carlsbad, California
London • Sydney • Johannesburg
Vancouver • Hong Kong • New Delhi

*To my dear friends John Rohan
and Stan Zemanek for believing in me!*

*To my very special and loving family
for supporting me!*

*And to my darling brother Kevin
who walks beside me.*

ACKNOWLEDGEMENTS > I would like to thank the following people, as without them this book would not be in your hands.

Firstly I would like to acknowledge Leon Nacson for taking on this project and Heidi Sullivan, both from Hay House. Their professionalism and support have been outstanding, and I thank them for their positive talks, meetings and for being on my wavelength. I have enjoyed working with them immensely and feel I have made two great new friends.

To the world's best editor Serene Conneeley, for being herself and so much fun to work with.

To Leela at Spheres the Spirit Guide, the best magazine in Australia, for supporting and promoting me with my column and introducing me to Hay House.

To entertainer and actor John Rohan, who introduced me into the radio and media world, which has been a wonderful and exciting experience, and his partner Lorraine for her ongoing support.

I would also like to acknowledge 2UE's Stan Zemanek for having so much confidence in me, having me on his radio and television shows and always promoting my club shows and weekly stars to his large audience, and for acknowledging my accuracy with his predictions. And John Kerr at 2UE, who helped me along the way with spots on his show that led to many TV appearances.

I would like to acknowledge radio station 2UE for giving me such a wonderful opportunity with my own radio show, which eventually led to the demand for a book by the listeners and this book opportunity.

Special thanks to my wonderful mum and dad, and my sister and best friend Cathy and her daughters Olivia and Cassie and husband Steve, who are always there to listen to my ideas and give me such wonderful encouragement.

And to my husband Chris and gorgeous little son Liam for loving me and making me proud.

FORTUNE TELLING AND DIVINATION MADE EASY > Everyone has the power to see what the future holds. The ancient art of fortune telling is a vast subject with enough history, myth and instructions to fill scores of weighty tomes. The aim of this little book is to provide an introduction to the art of divination and psychic development, and give you some fun, everyday ways to predict your future.

You will discover how to give psychic readings and to divine information using common and inexpensive household items such as tea leaves or coffee grounds, a pack of playing cards, candles, a pair of dice or a bowl of water or ice. It doesn't really matter what you use for divination – it is simply a tool to help you use and develop your own intuition. And the more you use this book, the better you will become and the more you will start to trust that inner voice we all have inside.

I personally feel that when you relax you tune in best, so don't stress about the outcome. Just have fun, and know that you have the potential to predict your own future. Try practising on your family, your friends, your work colleagues and especially yourself as much as you can, because the more you do it the better you will become and the more your intuition will develop.

When reading for others, keep in mind that it is better to give someone a positive reading. Even if your instincts tell you that things are not looking too good for them, always be subtle and give them some hope, because I believe it is in the power of the mind to change our own destinies and manifest our own futures by staying as positive as possible. We also have the ability to change negative thoughts into positive ones, and to create the life we want.

On a more serious note, don't try to predict serious health or legal problems, as this is best left to the professionals in those fields…

Enjoy!

CONTENTS >

Air reading	> 1
Car registration divination	> 9
Cheeky predictions	> 16
Chinese oracle	> 23
Colour reading	> 31
Crystal divination	> 37
Dice throwing	> 44
Doodling	> 49
Envelopes of destiny	> 56
Face reading	> 59
Feet reading	> 70
Feng shui	> 77
Fire reading	> 85
Flower predictions	> 92
Food divination	> 102
Food for your mood	> 108
Hand games	> 114
Hand writing	> 119

Head reading	> 127
I Ching made easy	> 143
Mole readings	> 164
Numerology	> 171
Omens	> 182
Palmistry	> 192
Pendulum	> 209
Playing cards	> 216
Psychic animals	> 226
Runes	> 237
Scrying	> 244
Tablets of Fate	> 249
Tea leaf reading	> 272
About the author	> 281

AIR READING > Known as aeromancy, air reading is a type of divination determined by interpreting atmospheric conditions. It has been around since the beginning of time, as ancient civilisations placed great store in portents they divined from the weather and the celestial bodies of the heavens. There are a few different methods of using this form of seeing the future, such as interpreting cloud shapes, studying the wind, thunder, lightning or shooting stars, and even observing the movement of air from a fan. The word aeromancy comes from the Greek aero, meaning "air", and manteia, meaning "divination".

AIR READING

CLOUD DIVINATION > Nephomancy, which is divination by interp-reting the shapes of clouds, has been used for centuries to gain insight into the future. If you're feeling in the mood and totally relaxed, sit outside and watch the clouds. What do the shapes look like to you? Here are some possible cloud formations and their meaning, although your own interpretation of the meaning of the shapes gives extra insight, so keep a journal and develop your own dictionary of symbology.

Angel >	Spiritual guidance or messages are coming from above – be alert.
Ballerina >	Enjoyment and fun are coming back into your life.
Cat >	Your intuition is very strong right now, so listen to your inner voice.
Child >	You will get great enjoyment out of the simple things in life – kicking a ball around,

AIR READING

acting childlike and fancy free – and have the time of your life.

Crocodile >	There is danger and deception ahead, so be careful.
Deer >	You are too easygoing – stand up for yourself and stop burying problems under the carpet.
Dog >	Loyal friends are currently in your life, so make sure you appreciate them.
Dove >	Love vibes are extremely strong right now – this is an excellent cloud shape for singles.
Dragon >	The ultimate power cloud! You're about to go for gold and conquer your fears.
Duck >	A journey over water is in your future. You

	will also have to make decisions regarding your relationships and emotions.
Eagle >	The cloud of a winner. Goals will be reached and success attained. You're on top of the world!
Feather >	You will overcome difficult situations and obstacles. Travel is also likely.
Horse >	You'll be galloping to success, following your dreams and seeing your wishes come to fruition.
Leopard >	This indicates that you have the courage to survive anything life throws your way.
Polar bear >	You will no longer sit on the fence – it's full steam ahead, with you facing problems head on and being decisive and fearless.

AIR READING   >5

Rabbit >	This shape can indicate an upcoming pregnancy, or news of the birth of a child.
Sheep >	You have big decisions and choices to make, but you mustn't follow others – decide your own direction.
UFO >	You are searching for higher intelligence or purpose and answers to life's big mysteries.

ANSWER FROM ABOVE >

Here is an easy way to use air reading, or aeromancy.

1 > Think of a question that has a yes or no answer.
2 > Get two pieces of paper of the same size, shape, colour and weight and write "yes" on one and "no" on the other.
3 > Screw each piece up into a ball, and either open a window and throw them out, or throw them high in the air and watch them fall.
4 > The one that lands first is your answer.

MULTIPLE ANSWERS >

If your question is more complex, try this exercise.

1 > Hold a question in your mind, close your eyes and think of every possible answer to the problem.

2 > Get enough pieces of paper of the same size, shape, colour and weight to write each possible answer on a separate piece. Write them down and lay them all flat on a table together.

3 > Turn on a fan, or if there is a breeze outside open the window. The first piece of paper that falls on the floor is your answer.

FOR FUN AND FORTUNE > To make this cute fortune telling kit, you need 12 pieces of cardboard all of different colours, but the same size, shape and weight (similar to a business card). Write the following predictions on the corresponding coloured paper. Take these cards with you whenever you need a quick answer. You can place them on your car seat and turn on the air conditioner, turn on the hairdryer or fan at home while sitting with the cards laid out on a table, or sit near a window at the office with the cards spread out nearby. The first one to fall off the table or out the window or on to the floor of the car is your answer.

Red >	Dynamic career or financial moves are coming in the near future.
Orange >	There are positive vibes around love and finances – you are energetic and ready for action.
Yellow >	Wonderful new friendships and good communication will be with you soon.
Green >	Take better care of your health.
Blue >	A peaceful time ahead awaits you.

AIR READING

Purple >	Your spirituality is about to grow enormously through the testing period ahead.
Pink >	Romance is sizzling for you at this time.
Black >	Negative vibes, deception and temptation surround you – beware.
Grey >	You are feeling depressed or emotionally unfulfilled.
Gold >	Money is in abundance right now, so take advantage.
Silver >	A wish is about to come true.
Brown >	Now is the time to make long-term plans and real estate decisions.

CAR REGISTRATION DIVINATION > A modern method of divination is through your car registration. The numbers and letters on your car's number plate, or licence plate, can play a part in how lucky you are in life, love, money, career and family. And if you're in the market to buy a new car, check out the ones that have a number plate that adds up to eight to get the best of the lot.

To discover your car registration number, add up the letters in your number plate using the table over the page, where each letter corresponds to a number, then add the numbers of the plate to this figure. Keep breaking the number down until you get a single digit – if your total is 18, add 1+8 to get a final figure of 9.

CONVERT YOUR LETTERS >

1	2	3	4	5	6	7	8	9
A	B	C	D	E	F	G	H	I
J	K	L	M	N	O	P	Q	R
S	T	U	V	W	X	Y	Z	

EXAMPLES >

> AUE 130

1+3+5=9 and 1+3+0=4, so add 9+4, which equals 13, then 1+3, which equals 4. Your car registration divination number is 4.

> RHQ 896

9+8+8=25 and 8+9+6=23, so add 25+23, which equals 48, then 4+8, which equals 12, then 1+2, which equals 3. Your car registration divination number is 3.

WHAT DOES YOUR NUMBER MEAN? >

ONE > You're going to be more assertive and bold if you're driving around with this number. You're also more likely to take risks, so be careful as this applies to the freeways as well as to your life. You will feel more independent with this vibration, especially if the car is red – which could also attract more speeding and traffic fines than most.

TWO > The need for peace is more apparent with this number – you try to avoid confrontations where you can, and will be a considerate and patient driver. This car must be kept clean at all times to get the best out of it and your life. You will attract many admirers if single, and this is a great number plate for promoting good family or love vibes, and a good one to drive a baby in.

THREE > This is a fun number, and you will attract lots of social activity if your car has this vibration. It is an excellent number for those in the entertainment field, as it means you will be driving to lots of fun destinations. Your life will be filled with laughter and good communication – although having a green car with this number plate is the least likely to bring you good luck and capitalise on the vibration.

FOUR > You will attract more passion into your life if you're driving around in a car with this number. It will also help you feel more able to make long-term plans, and bring you opportunities to pay off any debt through lots of hard work. To enhance the vibration of this number, a white or silver car is best.

FIVE > Everything will be exciting and a little chaotic while you drive this car. People will be coming and going, and there will be places to see and lots of travel. There will be new connections too, and little time to rest. There will be lots of restless energy surrounding you when driving, so be careful not to go too fast or drive recklessly, and you'll feel the need for change.

SIX > This is a great family number, so if you're looking for a family car this licence plate is desirable. Love vibes are also increased, so relationships will improve or you will be able to draw one to you if it is missing. You can enhance this number by having a pink car, wearing pink when driving or, if this is too much, simply keeping a rose quartz in the car.

SEVEN > If you drive a car with this number, there will be lots of analysing and deep thinking going on, and maybe even spiritual experiences. It's great for writers, journalists and spiritual workers. Your intuition will be high while driving, so it's good to plan your day while you're at the wheel. It may break down occasionally though, so keep it well serviced, and be careful while parking.

EIGHT > This is the best number of them all for a car! Many opportunities will come your way while driving a car with this licence plate number – it's the one I always choose to optimise all the good things in my life. Money will come to you, along with success and strength, if you take advantage of this great number vibration.

NINE > Your thirst for knowledge will be stronger while having a car with this number, so it's a great one to pick if you're a doctor, healer or teacher. It can also help bring about change in your life, and encourage travel. You will find you want to help people if you have this car registration though, so be ready to give your time and energy.

PREDICTIONS >

You can also predict the future when driving. Think of a question you want answered, then pull over for a minute, close your eyes and ask your question out loud. Open your eyes and focus on the car registration number of the first car you see driving by you. Add up its numbers in the same way you did before to find your answer.

1 > A fresh start. Great opportunities are approaching, so stay positive.
2 > A love relationship is about to reach a positive turning point, and there will be harmony in difficult relationships.

3 > A wish is coming true.

4 > A long-term decision will be made this week. Property matters also loom.

5 > Travel, excitement and new friendships are coming up.

6 > Love is set to sizzle – a passionate encounter awaits you. Ooh la la!

7 > You will experience obstacles and feel emotional, but this will eventually pass.

8 > You're in the money, honey!

9 > Reunions, long distance travel and new career directions are indicated.

CHEEKY PREDICTIONS > This is a much more modern form of divination, but your bottom can say a lot about your character and what type of person you are! Check out yours or your partners and use your imagination to decide the fruit that most resembles your rear end. *Note:* Some people's butt may be a mixture of more than one, so check out all the shapes. Your bottom may also change shape – and fruit type – if you diet, exercise or put on weight, and yes, you do take on different personality traits if this happens!

KIWI FRUIT >

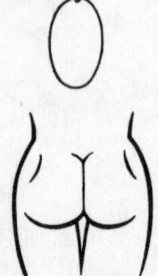

Example: Kylie Minogue and Brad Pitt. Someone with a small, firm, tight butt holds their emotions inside and runs on nervous energy. If they don't learn how to get those emotions out they could have disastrous love affairs, which start off strong but then end for no real reason. Drama is also more likely for this group. Soulmates are generally found later in life, but for people

CHEEKY PREDICTIONS   >17

who have learnt to communicate their innermost thoughts it's not uncommon to fall madly in love earlier on. Music and writing can help get their feelings out, and these personality types are very creative. High levels of stress can lead to health problems though, so it's very important for kiwi fruits to stay healthy, exercise regularly and eat correctly.

Best careers > Entertainment, hospitality, healing, nursing, psychic work, anything energetic.

PEAR >

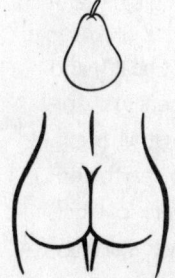

Example: Jennifer Lopez, Shane Warne. These people are very passionate about everything, and they make great lovers with the right person. They are very popular with the opposite sex, and can sometimes be led into temptation, so it will take a very special partner to keep them from becoming restless. If they are in a relationship that is unsatisfying they will try to make it work, but if that is impossible they will find someone else. They are very goal orientated and generally busy and successful in life. They love to display their wealth and success with a beautiful home, expensive car and jewellery. On a positive level they can be great mates, loyal friends, and lovers of family traditions and children.

Best careers > Self-employment, real estate, pub manager, organiser of all kinds, fashion industry, high flyer, acting. Fame often surrounds them.

BEAN >

Example: Ian Thorpe, Jamie Lee Curtis. These are the people with long flat butts that are lean and muscly. They are into fitness and know a lot about health and keeping themselves and others in shape. They can be a bit of a know it all, but they are very funny, down to earth and extremely loyal, as well as very loving and talkative. They are forever starting

CHEEKY PREDICTIONS > 19

something new, like exercise, a diet or a study course, but can lack the willpower to finish what's started unless they see success early on. If a guy has this shape it will take him forever to finish things around the home, despite his good intentions and vows to do it. In extreme cases some Beans are very tight with money.

Best careers > Comedian, taxation accountant, personal manager, fitness or diet industry, teacher, athlete.

WATERMELON > Example: Serena Williams, Luciano Pavarotti.

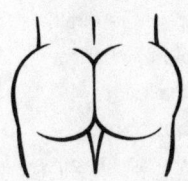

This is the butt where you see the person first then their bottom arrives 10 minutes later – a real sticker-outer. An extremely large version of this could indicate that the person doesn't eat correctly, and may develop health problems later in life. It's important for them to have a healthy diet, exercise regularly and lower their stress levels. However if their bottom is like Serena's, shapely and firm, they are sensual and enjoy all that life has to offer. Watermelon types are good listeners, ambitious but sometimes insecure. They hold a lot of other people's secrets, and are often misunderstood, so they must ensure they clarify their thoughts to others. They love music and have an excellent singing voice, and also love and appreciate family.

Best careers > Singer, music teacher, dressmaker, computers, travel agent, bank or loans officer, manager.

PEACH >

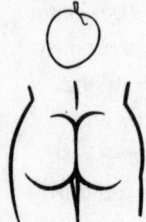

Example: Angelina Jolie, George Clooney. This type loves harmony and is well balanced with an even temper. Generally optimistic, they are adaptable to change, and need excitement and challenges otherwise they could become bored. These people may appear shy and reserved

CHEEKY PREDICTIONS > 21

around love matters, but watch them – they are highly sexed with the right partner, and when their fire is lit you will see "do not disturb signs" on their bedroom doors. Peaches are honest, with traditional values, but can be people pleasers at times. They are also excellent soft manipulators, selling ideas without looking like they are selling anything. They often accumulate a lot of wealth, but they are true humanitarians, and are very kind to those less fortunate than themselves.

Best careers > Charity organisers, promotional office, police force, doctor, medicine, vet, designer, pilot, real estate.

ORANGE >

Example> Madonna, Bill Clinton.

This butt is perfectly rounded, and can be small or large. These people like to be busy, and attract many friends in high places as well as people from all walks of life. They are charismatic, highly talented and excellent communicators, but most of all hard working. They have good staying power and lots of energy, but know when enough is enough. They can fall into depression though if they don't have lots of support around them, and must learn to stay clear of negative, jealous people who try to pull them down. Their choice of partner is very important as they can't stand clinging vines. They desperately need their freedom, and some are very childlike, never wanting to grow up. But if they find a partner willing to give them enough independence they will be spontaneous and fun and will have a very joyful union with them. They do not tolerate fools and have a very shrewd business sense.

Best careers > Politics, professor, event organiser, corporate flyer, travel industry, self-employment, restaurant owner, fashion designer, hairdresser.

CHINESE ORACLE >

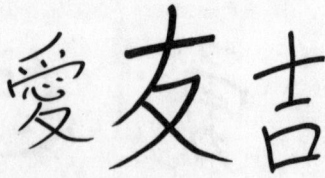

This beautiful oracle, based on an ancient Chinese method, can easily be used for divination. Just close your eyes, turn this book around three times then, with your eyes still closed, stick a pin or your finger on to the page. Open your eyes and see which oracle you have selected, then read below for the meaning.

LUCKY >

This tells of great fortune and success coming your way soon. Do not hold back – be bold and daring and go for gold. This is also a good omen for those thinking about going for a new job or purchasing or selling property. If this is your aim, place nine river stones glued together then sprayed gold close to your front door.

FRIEND >

友

You have many new friendships about to form, will join new social groups and sporting activities, and your life will be enriched and full once again. You will be very popular, and your new friends will love and respect you. Place some yellow flowers or candles inside your home now to enhance the situation.

LOVE >

愛

Sizzling romantic vibes surround you now. A soulmate is close for singles, and those in a relationship may commit further. Your aura is dynamite, and you are feeling and looking sexier than ever. New family members through births or marriages are also likely. Place happy photos of yourself and your family around the home.

FORGIVENESS > You need to let go of past hurts and disappointments and realise that they are just part of your learning so that you can move on and grow personally. Emotional baggage has been affecting your health, so face up to this now rather than sweeping problems under the carpet, so that you can close the doors forever.

BEAUTIFUL > You need to be reminded of how beautiful you are, as you don't feel too confident in yourself right now. Give yourself a mini makeover – get healthy and fit so you feel your best, and splurge on a new piece of clothing or a haircut if you can. A tiny attitude adjustment and some positive affirmations will have you feeling and looking your best at every opportunity.

CHINESE ORACLE > 27

KINDNESS >

A small sacrifice or kind act you do for someone else will really speed up your spiritual growth, so if someone needs your help, try to give what you can. Charitable work is also likely at this time, and will be rewarding for you. Helping people less fortunate than yourself makes for a happier and more fulfilling life.

LONGEVITY >

This indicates that it is time to wake up to yourself and take better care of health concerns, of either yourself or someone close to you. You have to stop stressing and start relaxing more – meditating and being out in nature is ideal. Place a picture in a green frame on your wall or plant a herb garden or fruit trees in the garden to help you affirm your good health.

PROSPERITY >

禄

You will have excellent opportunities for increasing your finances in the coming six months, and will achieve financial security. You are also able to make many long-term plans and decisions at the moment, and if you're prepared to put in the work you will be rewarded accordingly. Place three Chinese coins on your key ring and a small crystal ball beside your computer.

WISDOM >

智

Someone very wise is about to give you sound advice about your future, so consider all that people are telling you and pay attention to anything that applies to you. This could also represent legal issues with pleasing outcomes. Listening to other people's wisdom will see your life change for the better.

CHINESE ORACLE

WEALTH >

財

A win of some kind is indicated now. You will also be lucky in love, so stay positive and get rid of clutter in your home, car and office, as this will symbolically create space for new opportunities to come into your life. To enhance these vibrations, place a jade plant or money tree at your front door.

PEACE >

和

Peace is exactly what is on its way to you now – there will be a restful time after a period of doubt and confusion. A clearer vision of your future direction will also be shown. Place a picture or symbol of two doves in your home to enhance this. Your intuition is also very strong right now, so look for the messages coming from other planes.

COURAGE >

You will have the stamina, strength and vitality needed to overcome all the problems, obstacles and decisions in your life right now. Stand up and fight for what you want or what is yours, as the universe will support you at this time. Wear something red if you are feeling vulnerable, and know that you are a survivor no matter what.

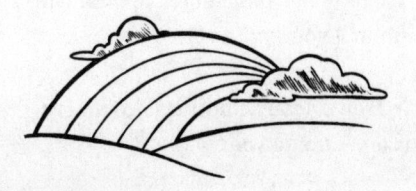

COLOUR READING >

CRAFTY COLOURED PREDICTIONS > Colours all have their own unique vibration, and can affect you and your future. For guidance or a mini psychic reading, create this cute colour oracle. Go to a newsagency, craft shop or hardware store that has paint sample cards. Cut out small business card sized cards in the following colours: red, orange, yellow, green, blue, purple, pink, white, black, gold and silver. Place them in a small bag for safe keeping, with a crystal of your choice. When you feel the need to answer a particular question, close your eyes and select a card from the bag. Following is the meaning of each coloured card and thus the answer to your question.

RED > You will have success with career and/or money problems. There is also passion for singles, with electric love vibes surrounding you.

ORANGE > Tremendous emotional fulfilment, great joy and celebrations are coming your way.

YELLOW > New friendships are close by, and communication is excellent now.

GREEN > You need healing, relaxation and time out. Being in wide open spaces will help as this is a time to reassess your priorities.

BLUE > You're feeling emotional and depressed, but there are decisions to be made. Plan your future now to ensure a positive turn around.

PURPLE > Your intuition is very strong right now, so rely on your gut feelings and hunches.

PINK > There is family happiness, commitment and a soulmate connection for you – your aura will now attract more love into your life.

WHITE > A cleansing of your emotions is occurring. Work on letting go of past hurts so you can move forward with your life.

BLACK > Beware of deception, and decide who you can trust with your innermost secrets or plans – keep them closely guarded and take care.

GOLD > This indicates bliss, kicking goals, the ultimate opportunities and wishes coming true.

SILVER > A psychic awakening is taking place, and you are becoming more spiritual and learning new skills.

COLOUR YOUR WORLD >

While you can divine and predict your future with colour, you can also utilise it to influence your life in a positive way and change its outcome. Colour has a huge effect on your mood, so dressing in certain colours can attract different things into your life and make you feel more confident in a certain area. Check out our table to see which colours to wear to attract the things you want.

Love >	Wear all shades of pink up to a light pinky red, but avoid maroon or terracotta.
Passion >	Red and hot pink are red-hot for lovers, while wearing pale pink is also good for lighting up a dull love life.
Wealth >	Purple or red will attract more money than other colours, so wear them whenever you are feeling financial strain.

COLOUR READING

Success >	Wear red as it is a powerful colour – unless you have red hair, in which case you should wear purple, as too much red can make you a little aggressive.
Happiness >	Dress in yellow, orange or apricot shades to draw joy to you and lift your mood.
Job success >	Choose red or yellow, even if it is just a coloured trim on a white jacket or a brightly hued shirt under a black suit.
Calm >	If you are feeling hyperactive, wear apple green, as it promotes happiness and wellbeing. If you are stressed, wear blue to calm you down.
Psychic insight >	Choose any shades of purple, and avoid bright colours. Silver accessories or clothing can also help.

COLOUR READING

Confidence >	If you are feeling insecure or intimidated, wear gold.
Grounding >	Wear brown as it will ground you and help you make sense of what you are looking for.
Decisiveness >	Wear orange, even just as underwear or as an accessory, and a little flash of gold to help you make important decisions.
Health >	Wear green, which is also good for harmonising any troublesome situations.
Creativity >	Wear orange or yellow to come up with new ideas and enhance your creativity.
Safe travel >	Wear blue and green to protect you as you travel, and tie a bit of turquoise around your suitcases to add to the effect.

CRYSTAL DIVINATION > Crystals are great for physical and emotional healing, and they are also excellent tools for making predictions for the future. For a simple divination, close your eyes and use your finger or a pin to point to a stone, on the table overleaf, then read its meaning on the following pages. To create your own crystal oracle, collect a small piece of each of the crystals listed and keep them in a purple chiffon bag, available at any craft store. Then whenever you are in need of answers and guidance, simply select a crystal from the bag and read its meaning. To boost the power of your future, keep the crystal close to you for the next week to take advantage of its vibrations.

38 < CRYSTAL DIVINATION

Clear quartz	Tiger's eye	Rose quartz	Aventurine
Ametrine	Tektite	Chrysocolla	Carnelian
Hematite	Smoky quartz	Agate	Fluorite
Bloodstone	Kunzite	Kyanite	Emerald
Citrine	Black tourmaline	Moonstone	Black onyx

CRYSTAL DIVINATION > 39

Agate >	This indicates new directions. Now is the time to take risks and be assertive, bold and daring. Do not hold back.
Ametrine >	It's decision time! Don't worry though – you will make progress and can transform and reinvent yourself for the better. Embrace a new outlook.
Aventurine >	You'll have a sudden change of luck – things are working in your favour and money opportunities surround you. Make the most of this now.
Black onyx >	Be careful of foolish mistakes at this time. Temptation may run riot, and singles should be on guard against deception and lust.
Black tourmaline >	This indicates endings and transformation. Doors are closing, so let go of the past and

walk through them, shutting them behind you, and embrace this chance to move forward.

Bloodstone > This is a time to find balance in your life, as there is a need for more harmony. You also have the ability to move on from people who have proved to be false.

Carnelian > This stone can indicate a pregnancy for yourself or someone close to you, or spending blissful time with family. Your business will also prosper right now.

Chrysocolla > Be on your guard, as there is the potential for chaos, destruction, unforeseen peril and emotional upheaval at this time.

Citrine > You are strong right now, and able to solve problems and improve difficult situations

	or relationships. You have the confidence to make necessary changes to your life now, so take advantage of it.
Clear quartz >	You have the ability to solve your own problems at this time. Do some meditation with this crystal and find your own answers within.
Emerald >	A person in authority – it could be your father or a father figure – is offering his help and sound advice. Listen carefully as there is wisdom here.
Fluorite >	It's a time for soul searching. Review your life, looking at past mistakes and decisions, and ponder the right choices for the future. A better way of living is opening up for you.

CRYSTAL DIVINATION

Hematite > This can represent marriage, graduation or family celebrations. You will feel a warm sense of belonging and fulfilment.

Kunzite > You are surrounded by peace and harmony at this time. You will enjoy excellent communication and spiritual insight, but be patient.

Kyanite > Your future direction is about to be revealed, so watch for the signs. Any doubts and confusion will soon pass, so relax and enjoy life.

Moonstone > Your intuition is very high right now, so rely on your gut feelings and thoughts and pay attention to your dreams, which may be more intense.

CRYSTAL DIVINATION > 43

Rose quartz >	You're facing a choice between love and career, or it could be a choice between two lovers. There are temptations, and passions will run riot.
Smoky quartz >	Take time out to think things through and reassess. You're feeling disappointed by past experiences – work out why so you can move on.
Tektite >	A wish is about to come true, so make one on the next star you see!
Tiger's eye >	The sun is shining on you now. There will be career and business growth, fabulous communication in relationships, growth and new-found optimism.

DICE THROWING > Dice throwing is a type of sortilage, which is a form of divination made by the casting of lots. It has been popular since ancient times, although in the past things such as animal bones (remember the kids' game knuckles?) were used, as well as twigs and stones. Dice have also been used for centuries, and some cultures even created them with 14 sides, to give far more specific predictions. A dice can have any number of sides, although the most common is six, and throwing two or even three gives a more comprehensive set of options and interpretations. To try this method, simply find a dice from a board game, buy one or even make your own. Then just roll it and read the meaning listed to see what is coming up for you, or ask a question as you roll to get guidance on a specific issue.

DICE THROWING > 45

- This indicates fresh starts and brand new opportunities. It's a time to be assertive, bold and daring and go for what you want career-wise or personally. The time is also ripe for romance, and career promotions for those who stay positive.

- It's a time of slow growth and important decisions regarding existing friendships and partners. Take your time and choose wisely. There may be emotional upheavals to deal with – although romance for singles is likely, so enjoy!

- If you asked about love, this number indicates that a commitment or celebration is close by. There are also excellent career and money vibes around you now, and you'll have fun with social activities and valuable new connections both personally and professionally.

[4] This reveals tough and trying times and the need to make long-term decisions. Try to stay away from negative people as they have the power to destroy your confidence. Lots of spending is also indicated, and it's a good time for buying or selling.

[5] There's a big change of direction coming, and it's for the better. Communication will be smooth, and there is excitement and action surrounding you. It's an ideal time to meet someone new or inject passion back into existing relationships.

[6] You'll be attracting people like a magnet from now on, and the drought is over for those searching for love. There may be new family members through marriage or births, and there are also excellent work and career vibes, especially for those who are self-employed.

DICE THROWING

ASTRAGALOMANCY > This is a form of divination involving two dice, which can help you with the answer to a specific question – a little like the modern Magic 8 Ball. Simply draw a circle on a piece of paper, concentrate on your question, and throw two dice together so they land in the circle. Add the numbers from the two dice – although if one falls outside the circle it is not counted, so your answer will be from 1-6.

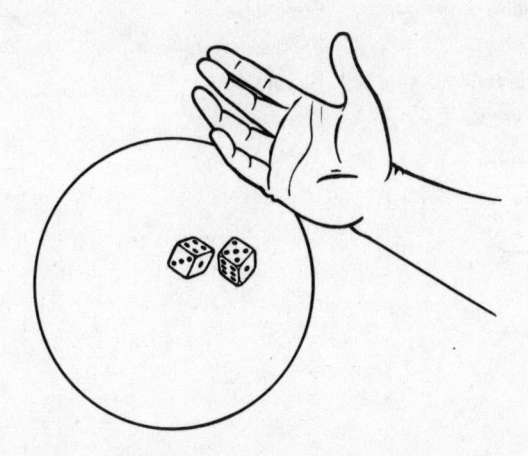

> **One**	=	Yes.
> **Two**	=	No.
> **Three**	=	Be careful.
> **Four**	=	Listen to advice.
> **Five**	=	You need some luck for this one!
> **Six**	=	Absolutely!
> **Seven**	=	Trust.
> **Eight**	=	Have patience.
> **Nine**	=	Definitely.
> **Ten**	=	Probably not.
> **Eleven**	=	No way!
> **Twelve**	=	Possibly.

DOODLING > The doodles you idly draw while you're on the phone or not paying attention in class can reveal a lot about your state of mind and even whether you're relaxed enough to predict your future. Clear your mind and start doodling, then examine what you drew and decode the meaning. If you can find some past or even recent doodles look them up too, because interpreting them will give you insight into your state of mind at that time, and will be even more indicative of your feelings as you weren't pre-empted.

Circles >	You are feeling emptiness in one part of your life. If the circle is completely joined you will feel great contentment and fulfilment soon, and more than one circle indicates a wish coming true.
Triangles >	You're intelligent and will learn a new skill shortly. You don't need any help solving the problems you face at the moment – you can do it yourself.
Squares >	Security is uppermost in your mind right now, along with making financial and long-term decisions. You are scared to take risks at this time, but there is a big financial opportunity coming.
Swirls and open curves >	Psychic experiences are likely around you now, and you will be receptive to them. Your intuition is extremely high at this time,

and an awakening to a more spiritual level will take place soon.

Flowers > These indicate lots of love and emotional fulfilment in your life. There is also good news around finances or on the work front, and you may enjoy surprises and gifts.

Angels > You are receiving spiritual guidance from above, so look for symbols and signs around you. It can also mean a deceased loved one is trying to get a message to you, so pay attention to what people tell you, as the wisdom could come to you through someone else.

Hearts > If there is one big one on the page a new love affair is about to begin, ooh la la! If there are two hearts, this can mean a proposal is imminent. If there are three hearts, the birth of a child is in the near future. If the heart is heavily drawn, over and over, then heartache is surrounding you – the healing will begin when you learn to let go.

Stars >

One big star indicates that a major wish will come true. If the stars are smaller and to the left side of the page then a missed opportunity happened in the past. If the stars are on the right side, many wishes will start to come true from now on.

Sun >

The sun represents energy, and shows that you have a new-found optimism for the future. Surround yourself with loved ones and positive people to make the most of what this wonderful doodle reveals.

DOODLING > 53

Initials or numbers >	Generally these indicate people who are about to come into your life, especially if they are in the middle of the page or to the right. If they're on the left, someone is about to return to your life, and there are reunions galore. If you drew an S in any shape or size, this is a fabulous omen for money gains.
Dollar signs >	This shows money gains and opportunities around you.
Birds >	Drawing birds reveals a yearning for travel or an upcoming trip. Islands and maps of Australia or other countries also mean travel.
Question mark >	Drawing question marks on the page means you are facing decisions.

54 < DOODLING

Kings, crowns, royalty mark >	Fame is there for you in the future.
Chaotic patterns heavily pressured >	You're feeling aggressive, disappointed, vulnerable or jealous over a relationship currently in your life. Let go, as you're wasting your energy.
Arrows, or lots of straight, heavy lines >	This indicates a negative frame of mind. You have a lot of anger built up and are feeling a bit self-destructive, or have a lot of emotional baggage to let go of.
Any drawings with very heavy pressure >	This reveals frustration, irritation, sleepless nights and worries. There are endings around you, and you may be experiencing financial difficulties.
Doodles leaning to the right >	You're longing to travel and escape your present situation or relationship. If the

DOODLING > 55

penmanship is fairly heavy, big changes are in store.

Doodles leaning to left > You are dwelling too much in the past, reminiscing about happier times. If there are flowers within this doodle you are contemplating past loves. Move forward.

ENVELOPES OF DESTINY > If you're having a dinner party or a morning tea with friends, why not add a fortune telling aspect to it? Try some of the exercises in this book, like getting everyone to write a paragraph then analysing their handwriting, or have them choose their favourite flower so you can tell them what it says about them. You can also prepare the following fun exercise in advance.

PARTY FAVOUR FORTUNE >
Get three big envelopes and write the words
> LOVE
> FINANCE
> DESTINY
one on each envelope.

In each envelope place 12 or more predictions that are related to that topic. Make them as serious, funny or raunchy as you like, depending on the people who will be choosing them, and even add extra categories or change them if you like. You can get everyone to pick a category and then choose a fortune from that envelope, or they can pick one from each category and get a broader view of their future. Here are a few examples for each envelope. Make as many as you like – the more the better – and decorate them for extra appeal if you feel inclined.

LOVE >

> Passion is sizzling red hot – ooh la la!
> A new partner may soon enter your life for a short period of time.
> Watch out for temptations – you know what we mean!
> A proposal or offer around a personal relationship is approaching.
> Your soulmate may be found through a new course or hobby you take up.

- > Someone from the past will return and shake you up.
- > Are you jealous of one of your friends?

FINANCE >

- > Business opportunities are very close – go for it.
- > You'll have an increase in finances through a new project or money idea.
- > It's time to ask for a pay rise.
- > Lots of bills are indicated, so cut down on spending and stay away from those sales!

DESTINY >

- > There will be a new address for you in the next 12 months, so get ready to move.
- > Travel overseas is foretold.
- > There will be a big celebration within a month.
- > Joining a new exercise group will be really lucky for you.
- > A huge opportunity is approaching – don't let it pass you by.

Note: You can cover heaps of topics here to suit your guests and the situation.

FACE READING > Face reading, or physiognomy, means determining the personality of someone by analysing their facial features. The Chinese have been interpreting faces for centuries, claiming that different facial shapes and types correspond to various personality traits, and lately it has gained popularity in the western world too. Studying the face can help reveal whether a person is loyal and trustworthy – or selfish and vain – as well as their potential for love and success.

60 < FACE READING

FACE SHAPE >

OVAL > Friendly and intuitive, but can be lazy.

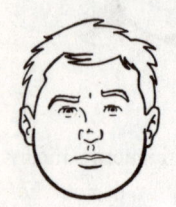

ROUND > Popular and creative, a good communicator and lucky in life.

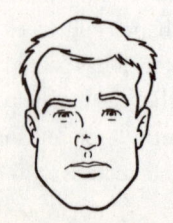

SQUARE > Active, strong, decisive.

FACE READING   > 61

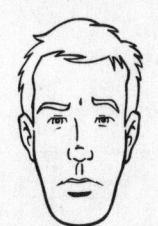

LONG > Patient, finishes what is started, traditional and generally successful.

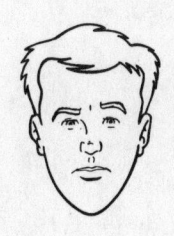

TRIANGULAR > *(wide forehead, pointy chin)* Smart, quick thinking, sometimes moody.

EYES >

Close set >	Calculating, responsible.
Wide set >	Can see the big picture. Confident, open minded.
Deep set >	Consider all sides, thoughtful.
Round >	Kind, honest, loving.
Almond >	Happy, sense of humour, shrewd.

Slanting >	Know what they want, can be secretive.
Bulging >	Smooth talker, can be bad tempered.

EYE COLOUR >

Brown >	Generous, compassionate, creative.
Grey >	Fun, spiritual, positive.
Green/grey >	Fun, happy-go-lucky type.
Blue >	Sweet, cheerful, loving.
Ice blue >	Can be calculating, selfish.
Green >	Passionate, ambitious.
Hazel >	Can be a pushover, need to learn to say no.
Black >	Ruthless, ambitious.

EYEBROWS >

Straight >	Ruthless, intense, creative, good sense of reasoning.
Curved >	Vulnerable, emotional, warm.

FACE READING

Angled >	Take charge, good leader.
Thick >	Powerful thinker, political – many leaders have them.
Thin >	Peacemaker, hold back, sit on fence.
Thick near nose, thin at end >	Very creative, but start projects they don't finish.
Thin near nose, thick at end >	Take a while to get going but are strong finishers.
Low brows >	Spontaneous, impatient, risk takers.
High brows >	Patient, slow moving, calm.
Middle brows >	Good reasoning powers, ability to see both sides.
Contradictory hairs >	Chaotic, love change, adventure and excitement.

MOUTH >

Wide mouth > Fun, great entertainer, good sense of humour, generous.

Narrow mouth > Sincere, excel with one to one conversations.

Big mouth > Generous, talkative, excitable, social, passionate.

Small mouth > Have trouble saying what they need to say.

Crooked mouth > Inner strength, ability to overcome challenges, may be deceitful.

Full lips > Sensuous and emotional, good communicators, charismatic.

Thin lips > Can be tight with money and emotions, more reserved.

Bigger bottom lip > Persuasive, good communicators, funny, popular.

Bigger top lip Honest, perceptive, courageous, but can be critical, selfish or vain.

Turned down lips > Pessimistic, negative, lazy and jealous of other people's success. But with the right influences and support, they can turn their life around to positive energy, so it's important who they choose as life partners.

NOSE >

Big and long >	Excellent with money, generally wealthy in life.
Short >	Can be a workaholic, impatient.
Thin >	Tight with emotions and money although generous with self.
Crooked >	Risk takers.
Small bulb >	Artistic, sporty, creative, good communicator.
Big bulb >	Financial security is very important.
Nose turns down >	Gullible, gossipy, can be negative.
Nose turns up >	Good business sense, an ideas person.
Thin nostrils >	Worry about security, good at sticking to budgets, bottle up feelings.

Large nostrils > Spendthrifts, good at juggling finances.
Flared nostrils > Excitable, fun loving, chaotic, changeable.

CHIN >

Protruding >	Independent, ruthless, determined, obsessive.
Rounded >	Common in successful, famous people.
Weak >	Indecisive.
Broad >	Sexy, survivors.
Long >	Indicates great staying power.
Prominent >	Competitive.
Small >	Hardworking, high moral standards.
Pointed >	Flirtatious, talented in music and dancing.
Square >	Grounded, security conscious, home lovers, inflexible.
Cleft >	Adventurous, friends from all walks of life, varied career paths.
Angled >	Need to stay in control of situations.
Curved >	Always put others first.
Dimpled >	Playful, childlike, cheeky.

FOREHEAD >

Wide >	Intelligent, practical, philosophical.
High and rounded >	Idealistic, friendship is important.
Narrow >	There are obstacles to success – persevere.
Protruding >	Daydreamers – concentrate on doing.
Flat >	Grounded and loyal.

EARS >

Large >	Receptive, switched on, alert, positive, energetic, generous.
Small >	Less receptive, can get easily bored.
Sticking out >	Good listeners who never miss out on the news.
Flat to head >	Selfish, only listen when interested.
Average >	A bit of both of the above.
Large lobes >	Independent, passionate.
Small lobes >	Sometimes lacking passion.
High ears >	Good debaters, impulsive, often interrupt.

Low ears >	Make strong decisions easily, expert at processing information.
Average >	Great listeners, good timing, can tune in to conversations easily.

TEETH >

Large >	Bossy, good leaders, like to be in control.
Small >	Busy, workaholic, security conscious.
Crooked >	Will have conflicts about major choices and decisions in life.
Big two front teeth >	Super achievers, strong, robust.
Small two front teeth >	Low self-esteem, need to be surrounded with upbeat people.
Space between front teeth >	Risk takers, dare devils, sometimes achieve fame.

Long sharp canines >	Have many lessons to learn.
Gaps >	Intuitive, successful, healthy outlook.

CHEEKS >

Big >	Determined, don't try to stand in their way!
Small >	Reserved, shy.
Well padded >	Supportive.
Hollow >	A survivor, generous, humanitarian, can be jealous.
High cheekbones >	Dramatic, talented, courageous, usually find fame of some kind.
Prominent >	Passionate, fast talking.
Close set >	Work extremely well and thrive under pressure.

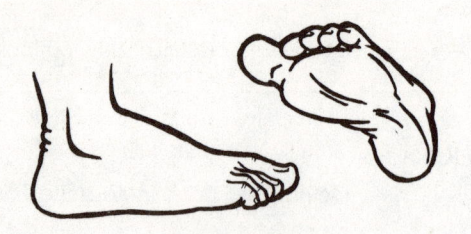

FEET READING > Just as the shape of your face can reveal things about your personality, so too can the shape of your feet. This can be a great tool for insight into new relationships, and you can read for friends and family or entertain people at a party.

FEET TEMPERATURES >
Warm feet >   Enthusiastic, energetic, really positive.
Cold feet >   Bored, weak, unmotivated, need to set goals.
Burning hot >   Anger is built up inside – need to let go or face up to problems.

FEET READING

FEET TYPES >

Large feet >	Doers, achievers, successful.
Small feet >	Gentle souls who tread lightly and take time making decisions.
Long thin >	Conservative, shy, keep emotions in, run on nervous energy.
Short wide >	Can be doormats, bad with finances.
Broad feet >	Fun loving, outspoken, people lovers, security conscious, grounded.
Floppy feet >	Need a confidence boost.
High arches >	Intelligent.
Low or flat arches >	Practical.
Swollen and puffy >	Emotional, psychic, but holding on to baggage. Need to let go.
Cracked heels >	Decisions need to be made when this happens.
Wrinkled feet >	Zapped of energy, need to drink lots of water and rest to prevent burnout.

FEET READING

| **Thick hard feet >** | Argumentative, strong willed, stubborn, need to lighten up. |

DETAILS ON FEET >

Right foot >	Past.
Left foot >	Future.
Line leading to second toe >	Marriage when young.
Lines at side of little toe >	The longer the line, the longer the relationship.
Lines leading to little toe >	Number of children.
Two lines leading to big toe >	Wealth, self-respect.
Curving lines >	Very creative and honest.
Vertical lines >	Can see both points of view.

FEET READING

Deep vertical line down foot >	Will probably do a lot of travel.
Two lines >	Will live in another country.
Lines across toes >	Experiencing a period of worry and anxiety.
White pockets beneath skin >	Reveal a collection of negative or angry thoughts.
Corns above toes >	Have faith and great belief in others.
Corns on the side of toes >	Need to listen to inner voice and gut feelings.
Corns below toes >	Can't make decisions.
Hard skin >	Uncertain about life.
Dents in foot >	Reveals a recent knockback.

HEEL PREDICTIONS >

Swollen >	Lacking energy, depressed.
Wrinkled, cracked >	Obstacles in the way, must face up to current challenges.
Cold >	Lacking confidence to let go of the past.
Painful >	May indicate sexual problems.
Hardened >	Stubborn, need to listen to others.
Smooth >	Ready for a new start and action.

TOE TYPES >

Long >	Energy in abundance.
Short >	Difficulty in expressing themselves.
Rounded >	Intelligent, sensitive, but can be taken advantage of.
Pointy >	Can be bad tempered.
Crooked >	Can indicate ill health.
Twisted >	Restless, finds it hard to commit.

FEET READING

Big toe stands apart >	Risk takers, loud, fun loving.
Longer big toe >	Self opinionated, like to be in charge.
Longer second toe >	Give what they receive. Very charitable.
Fat big toe >	Wealth comes after 30.
Fat second toe >	Wealth comes in the later part of life.
Red big toe >	Indicates feelings of anger, need to let go.
White big toe >	Get rest immediately.
Blueish big toe >	Ego has been damaged, need nurturing.
Flaking skin >	Frustrated and irritable.
Greenish tone >	Represents a moment of jealousy.
Yellowish >	Indicates happiness.

76 < FENG SHUI

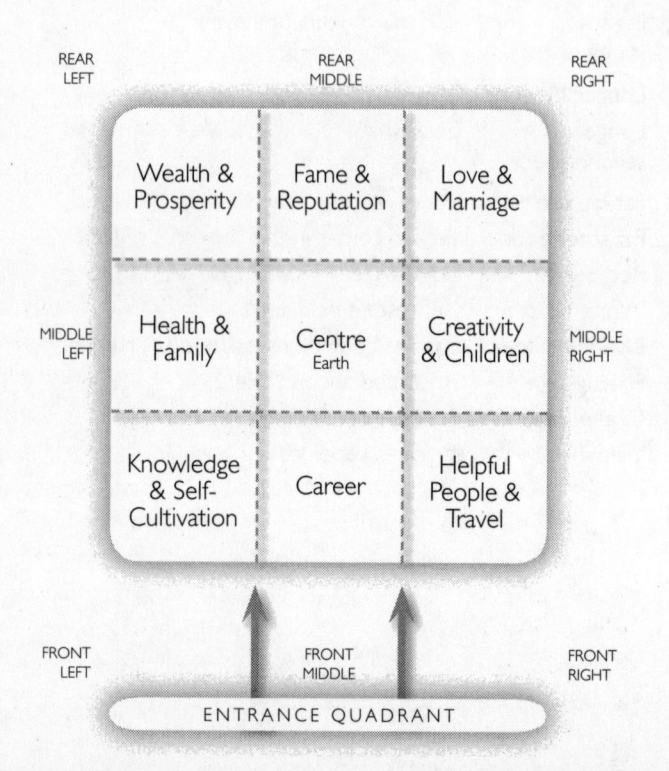

	REAR LEFT	REAR MIDDLE	REAR RIGHT
	Wealth & Prosperity	Fame & Reputation	Love & Marriage
MIDDLE LEFT	Health & Family	Centre Earth	Creativity & Children
	Knowledge & Self-Cultivation	Career	Helpful People & Travel
	FRONT LEFT	FRONT MIDDLE	FRONT RIGHT

MIDDLE RIGHT

ENTRANCE QUADRANT

FENG SHUI > Feng shui (pronounced foong shway) is the study of how to arrange your environment to enhance your life, and comes from an eastern philosophy relied on for more than 3000 years. It is based on the flow of energy throughout your house as well as the principles of the bagua map (see left), a grid that assigns qualities to different areas of your house.

To boost your happiness or success in a certain area, such as love, work out where that section is in your house and make sure there aren't any problems in that room that are stopping the harmonious flow of energy (chi) there. Simply removing the dead pot plant or flowers from your love area and replacing them with two red candles can change the energy of what you are drawing into your life. Removing clutter will also make a huge difference, as a congested house has very low chi, or energy, which means your life will be chaotic and stagnant, and you won't draw the beautiful people, harmony and positive opportunities to you that you should.

To map the feng shui in your place, draw a floor plan of your house and the rooms in it, as close to scale as you can. If the front door is not along the bottom of the grid, tip your plan accordingly so this occurs. Divide it into nine equal squares and superimpose the bagua map from the previous page on top. Standing in your front doorway, the love sector will be in the rear right-hand portion of the house, so whatever room is there is the one you have to concentrate on to boost your love energy. The one in the rear left-hand portion of the house is the wealth area, so be especially mindful of it if it's the bathroom or kitchen, as energy can literally go down the drains!

You can also use the map to do a mini-reading in every room in the house – for instance as you stand in the doorway to your bedroom, the far right corner looking in from the doorway is your love area, so make sure your dirty laundry basket isn't there!

And you can do the same from your back door, looking into the garden, to work out how your backyard is affecting you and your energy and emotions. Put a lively growing plant in the far left corner to increase your prosperity consciousness – and take notice of where you place a compost heap or a shed full of junk.

You can also stand at your front door looking out to the front garden and apply the bagua map in the same way. Place a pink flowering plant in the far right section to create better love prospects and harmony in existing relationships in your life.

TO IMPROVE FINANCES > Pay special attention to the room that falls in the finance area of the bagua map, at the rear left corner of the house. Clear out any clutter that could be inhibiting your wealth energy, and try some of these easy tips.

> Place a dragon picture or statue facing the door.
> Write out some wishes on paper and keep them in a gold box in the far left corner of the room.

- Place fish ornaments, pictures of fish or even fish in a bowl around the house. Round shaped ones like goldfish or carp are best – avoid sharp shaped ones like sharks or sharp finned fish as they are bad luck.
- Drink out of fish wine glasses, for drinking in the luck, or eat from bowls with fish painted on them.
- Keep three or eight goldfish in a large aquarium.
- Hang a picture of a rooster or have a small ceramic one in your kitchen.
- Place a jade plant outside your front door in a terracotta pot.
- Keep the toilet lid down so energy isn't flushed down the drain.
- Make a wish on a shooting star.
- Place fresh yellow flowers or pot plants around the home to attract prosperity.
- Be sure to get rid of clutter, and never have dead or dried flowers inside the home.

TO ATTRACT LOVE > Pay special attention to the room that falls in the love area of the bagua map, at the rear right corner of the house. Also ensure that your bedroom is peaceful and luxurious feeling. If you have a TV or exercise equipment in there hide them when not in use, as they disrupt the energy.

> Sleep on pink sheets.
> Place a rose quartz crystal beside the bed.
> Put a tiny round mirror under the mattress.
> Display two mandarin ducks in the living area.
> Hang pictures of family members or happy ones of yourself in the relationship area of the house.
> Have a crystal vase filled with fresh flowers.
> Tie Chinese coins on your key ring with red ribbon and put some under your front doormat.
> Sleep with a wedding ring (buy a cheap one) on your finger, and borrow a cup from a happily married friend to place it in during the day.

TO BOOST YOUR CAREER > Pay special attention to the room that falls in the career area of the bagua map, in the front centre of your house, which is often the entranceway. Also pay attention to your home office – apply the bagua map to this room too – or your desk at work.

- Place a small crystal ball on the far left side of your office desk.
- Keep eight small Chinese coins on your invoice book or diary.
- Put a rooster feather inside your desk for career advancement.
- Try to sit higher than everyone else in the office – raise your chair if possible.
- Sit in the power position at important meetings diagonally across from the door so you can see who enters.
- Do not sit with your back to the door.
- Dress your smartest at all times and have something red, such as a tie, scarf or wallet, with you.

TO INCREASE YOUR REPUTATION > Pay special attention to the room that falls in the fame and reputation area of the bagua map, in the rear centre of your house.

> Place pictures of people you admire and want to be like in this area.
> Have as much red, green or gold in the room as you can, whether it be a feature wall, statue, poster, ornament, curtains, or rug – whatever you can think of and feels good to you.
> If it's the bathroom or the kitchen, ensure drains are working properly and keep the toilet lid down – you don't want your reputation going down the drain!

TO IMPROVE YOUR HEALTH > Pay special attention to the room that falls in the health area of the bagua map, in the middle left of your house. Also ensure no area of your house is cluttered, as stagnant energy in the home can affect your physical wellbeing.

- Place a picture of yourself in a green frame in the health area.
- Plant a herb garden in the backyard or have a window box in the kitchen.
- For sore backs, place nine light coloured pieces of chalk under the bed.
- Put some uncooked rice in a little glass bowl and change it each day, visualising yourself getting better.

FIRE READING > Fire reading, or pyromancy, is divination by fire, and can be done by staring into a fire and interpreting the symbols in the flames as well as by watching the rate and pattern of the way things burn. It is an ancient form of divination, and was very common in civilisations where fire was revered and worshipped as a god or offerings were made to the gods by burning them. There are different kinds of pyromancy, including watching patterns in the smoke or flames of a fire, burning herbs, throwing leaves into a fire and seeing how they burn, passing a piece of paper through flames then interpreting the burn marks, and disrupting the flames to see how they react.

FIRE READING

ANSWERS IN THE FLAMES > Try this simple exercise to get the answer to a specific question. Sit before a fire and think of your question. Pass a plain white card through the fire three times while asking your question aloud. Take note of the smoke and flames as you do this, and look below to find the answer to your current situation.

> **Smoke rises straight up**	=	Yes!
> **Smoke hangs around heavily**	=	No.
> **Fire burns to one side**	=	A love wish will be granted.
> **Much crackling**	=	Challenges, losses and endings are indicated.
> **Hollow bit in middle of flame**	=	An end to problems is in sight.
> **Sudden roar and rise high**	=	Arguments and confrontations are imminent.
> **Three bolts of flame rise, burning separately**	=	A terrific omen of good fortune and a special event.

| > Fire starts to go out quickly | = | Your energy levels are low – do you need a health check-up? |
| > Fire takes off really fast | = | Opportunities and action abound, financial success is imminent. |

YES OR NO? > Sitting in front of a fire or barbeque, write out a question with a yes or no answer. Get two pieces of paper of the same size and shape but different colours and assign one as yes and one as no. While thinking about your question throw both pieces of paper into the flames. The first one to burn is your answer.

VISIONS IN THE FIRE > To see your future, let your mind go blank and your vision blur a little and stare into the flames of a fire. See if you can determine any patterns or visions, and use the list below – and your intuition – to determine the meaning of any symbols you see in the flames.

FIRE READING

Angel >	A period of sadness will be followed by great happiness and more support.
Animals >	You are about to form some good new friendships.
Axe >	This indicates endings.
Baby >	A birth, or the birth of a new project, is imminent.
Bed >	This can indicate affairs and secrets.
Book >	Their will be successful new endeavours and reflection of your life so far.
Castle >	Money is on the way.
Desk >	This can indicate a new job or a career change.

Fat person >	You worry too much about your image and have low self-esteem.
Feather >	A spiritual message is arriving soon – pay attention.
Frog >	This can indicate pregnancy for yourself or someone close to you.
Fruit >	Fruit shapes in fire mean creativity and abundance of money prospects.
Gate >	New doors are about to open for you, so let go of the past and move through them!
Grasshopper >	You have the freedom to do what you want in the future, and will have wonderful new adventures and reinvent yourself.

Hammer >	Hard work brings home the bacon – right now you need to put in more effort.
Hills, large >	There are challenges for you to overcome – the bigger the hills, the more there are.
Hills, small >	You are very close to your goals.
House >	A new address is likely for you.
Mask >	This is a common one for fire readings, and reveals that you are blocking out the real you or your true feelings.
Owl >	You will pass exams, study successfully, learn a new skill or do some self-improvement.
Paradise vision or shapes >	Terrific vibes surround you – tremendous happiness is very close.

People in a group >	A celebration is close by, such as a wedding.
Person's blurred shape >	Someone will be leaving your life.
Person's distinct shape >	Someone will enter your life in a favourable way very soon.
Sun >	You must accept responsibility for your own mistake.
Trees >	If there is one tree, it indicates a new friend is approaching. If there are two trees, it foretells a lover or commitment. If there are three trees, it shows a holiday to a tropical island.
Weapons >	Enemies are close so be careful.

FLOWER PREDICTIONS > Flowers can be used for healing and also for divination. To do a mini reading for yourself or someone else, close your eyes and turn the book around six times, then using a hairpin or pen, jab a spot, then open your eyes and see which flower you selected and read its meaning on the table opposite. You can also create an ongoing divination tool by drawing the flowers on to paper or cardboard and making your own flower oracle cards, selecting one whenever you want some guidance. Read the meaning of your favourite flower too, as it will give you insight into your inner self.

FLOWER PREDICTIONS > 93

Jacaranda	Sunshine wattle	Wisteria	Iris	Rose
Snapdragon	Gerbra	Chickweed	Daffodil	Bush fuchsia
Kangaroo paw	Lavender	Hibiscus	Dahlia	Silver princess
Black iris	Marigold	Tulip	Fringed violet	Lily
Fuchsia	Gardenia	Jasmine	Sunflower	Peony
Sturt Desert pea	Cinnamon	Catnip	Mountain devil	Primrose
Frangipani	Pansy	Bottlebrush	Peach flowered tea tree	Poppy

FLOWER MEANINGS >

Bush fuchsia > Your intuition is very high at this time. Rely on your gut feelings entirely, and pay particular attention to your dreams and instincts, as messages will be revealed within them.

Gerbra > You will have emotional upheavals to deal with, and major life changes are about to take place. Fascinating times are indicated!

Dahlia > A crucial decision surrounds you, and it is important that you make it this week. Weigh up your options, then be confident that you will make the right choice.

Tulip > Enormous power surrounds you right now – your aura is electric and you will kick huge goals and be very sociable.

FLOWER PREDICTIONS

Kangaroo paw > It's a time of growth for you now in all ways. You will be helping others, studying and learning new skills.

Daffodil > Growth in new businesses, climbing the ladder in your career and strengthening new-found relationships or friendships are all indicated. Sunshine is lucky, and so is yellow.

Sturt Desert pea > Sadness and emotional upsets are surrounding you at this time. Nurture yourself until it passes.

Sunshine wattle > This beautiful native flower indicates that a wish will come true, and there will be celebrations, good news, romance and money opportunities.

Fringed violet >	This is a flower of healing. There may be health concerns to be taken care of at this time, so look after yourself and don't ignore any physical twinges.
Jacaranda >	There are decisions to be made. This flower indicates that a change in direction and personal growth is ahead.
Rose >	Think romance and passion! Love is set to sizzle, and if you've had a love drought, it will soon be over.
Frangipani >	This indicates that you have the strength to cope in difficult times. There may be obstacles to overcome, but you will get through it.
Mountain devil >	Forgiveness is needed, so try to find it in your heart to let go of your pain and anger towards yourself or someone else.

FLOWER PREDICTIONS

Poppy > Reunions are likely in the coming weeks. This flower can also mean you'll be settling a difference or solving a problem once and for all.

Bottlebrush > The message of this flower is about letting go. It's time to move onwards to the future, so stop dwelling in the past, let go of your anger and allow yourself to shine!

Fuchsia > Invitations to glamorous events are likely in the near future, and you will meet dynamic new connections who will open your world up.

Lavender > If you're in a relationship, your sex life will be more passionate than ever, and singles could meet a red-hot new lover.

FLOWER PREDICTIONS

Peony > This is an excellent love flower, and indicates great joy and happiness in existing relationships and also for singles. You will experience pure joy.

Snapdragon > Travel plans are shaping up. This could also represent a change of address or job, so be prepared for excitement and new things!

Iris > Now is the time for acceptance of your life and past situations. This flower can also deepen your spirituality.

Peach flowered tea tree > A strong commitment will be made at this time.

Wisteria > Sexual energy surrounds you now and passion is oozing. Beware of temptations and cheaters however.

FLOWER PREDICTIONS > 99

Chickweed >   A pregnancy is likely for yourself or someone close to you, or you could get a new family member through marriage.

Gardenia >   A new friendship or romance is about to enter your life and lift your spirits.

Jasmine >   A spiritual journey is about to unfold. Your intuition is strong, and a soulmate experience awaits you.

Cinnamon >   If a man chooses this one it indicates that he will be more interested in passion than ever, but if a woman picks this it could mean she is experiencing a drought in the passion stakes.

Pansy >   New doors are about to open. It is a time for decluttering your life, moving on and the acceptance of past mistakes.

Marigold >	Wonderful new friendships are forming and there are soulmate connections around you. You're communicating brilliantly and your aura is charismatic.
Silver princess >	New goals are about to be realised and new friendships will be formed. This could also indicate travel.
Catnip >	This is a time to march on fiercely. No mountain is too big to climb – you're on a roll and will ride the wave all the way to huge success.
Hibiscus >	A romantic dinner or trip for two is indicated, so relax and enjoy yourself.
Lily >	This reveals bad luck around finances if care is not taken, so be aware. There is also

	an interesting stranger entering your life as a potential love interest or friend.
Primrose >	The potential for marriage is extremely high right now, and making deep commitments in work and career are also likely.
Black iris >	A relationship will finally come to an end – but don't despair, because this is for the best for all concerned.
Sunflower >	Your aura is sizzling and you seem to be more attractive to the opposite sex than ever, so use this time to your advantage. Singles could meet their soulmate shortly.

FOOD DIVINATION > There are heaps of old superstitions, omens and psychic indications surrounding food and what it means concerning your future. Here are a few sweet old beliefs, plus some new ways to divine your fortune or provide you with guidance, right in your kitchen or at the supermarket.

SWEET FORTUNE TELLING > If you're out and need a quick divination, just buy a packet of Smarties or M&M's. Tip them into a bowl or just open the packet. Close your eyes, think of your question and pull one out without looking. Its colour will give you your answer.

| FOOD DIVINATION > 103

> **Red** = This indicates victory and dynamic love.
> **Orange** = Great new business connections or new personal friends will form.
> **Yellow** = You'll feel a lot happier and more positive soon.
> **Green** = Look after your health.
> **Blue** = Slow down and try to be patient.
> **Brown** = Security will be yours soon, with opportunities to increase your finances.

Then have fun eating them!

CAKE DIVINATION > Mix up the ingredients for a cake, and just as you're about to put it in the pan to cook, stir in some pure silver charms such as horseshoes and fish. Cook as usual then slice up and hand to your guests. The charm they find in their slice of cake will indicate their fortune.

> **Horseshoe** = Good luck.
> **Fish** = Fertility and abundance.
> **Ring/circle** = Marriage.

> **Bird** = Flight and freedom.
> **Dolphin** = Strong intuition and spiritual growth.
> **Plane** = Travel.

You can also make your own fortune cookies by slipping coated paper with messages on it into each cookie, or charms as above. You can also choose your own symbols and intuitively divine the meanings yourself.

LOVE ANSWERS >
For guidance with your love life, just use these fruit and vegies!

> Throw an orange in the river and you will find a good husband in the near future. Or when shopping, think of romance and buy some pre-bagged oranges. Count them when you get home – if there is an even number you will find love soon, if it's uneven you'll remain single for now.

> Place a big bowl of oranges in the kitchen. Throughout the bowl hide little cards with your hopes and dreams

written on them, eg on separate cards write "love", "money", "friendship", "good health" – one or two words on each slip of paper is enough. When you eat your breakfast, close your eyes and take an orange and a card. Keep that card in your wallet until the wish comes true.

> Plant carrots in your garden. If the plants thrive so will your luck with romance, but if they don't grow, bad fortune will be yours for now.

> Eat bananas and avocadoes while thinking of your lover, or visualise a new one coming your way, and watch your sex life pick up in the near future.

> To find out when you'll marry (or any other big event), grab a bunch of cherries or grapes and place them one by one into three piles. The first is "this year", the second is "next year", the third is "not for a while". Keep placing them in the three groups until you reach the last one – whichever group your last cherry goes in is your answer.

> Thinking about marriage, take an apple and peel it. If you peel the whole apple in one piece, without breaking the peel, your wedding wish will soon be granted.

> Cut an apple in two and count the seeds. If there is an even amount you will marry, but if it's an odd number you'll stay single.

YES OR NO? >

If you need an answer to a yes or no question, try these two natural methods.

> Hold an apple with its twig still attached in your left hand. Ask a question that has a yes or no answer. As you hold the twig in your right hand, twirl the apple around, repeating yes, no, yes, no until the twig breaks. There is your answer.

> Take a healthy lettuce leaf, then write your question on a piece of paper. Place it on top of the lettuce and put it back

in the fridge. If the leaf remains healthy for a few days your answer is favourable to the question. If the leaf wilts straight away the answer is no.

TOO MANY OPTIONS >

Here are two interesting ways to find guidance when your question has several possible answers.

> To find an answer to a complex question, try onion divination. Write every possible answer to your question on a separate piece of paper, then stick each slip of paper on a different onion. Leave them to sprout – the first one to do so has your answer.

> Buy five pots for the kitchen windowsill and fill with dirt. Place herb seeds in each one, then write out your hopes and wishes for the future, either in black texta on each pot, or write each one on a different piece of paper and tape each one to a different pot. The first seed that germinates will reveal your answer to you.

FOOD FOR YOUR MOOD > Heard the expression "feeling blue"? Maybe you feel aggro and are "seeing red"? Foods affect us emotionally and spiritually, and not just with their nutritional content. Colour also has an impact on your psyche, so combine these two aspects and change your life!

RED FOODS > Need to be bolder? Want more energy? Is passion lacking? People who eat a lot of red foods are generally lean and physically active with quick movements and lots of confidence. And lycopene, found in tomatoes, is thought to fight off cancer forming toxins. For extra confidence, wear red too.

Great red foods: Strawberries, cherries, asparagus, leafy green vegies, plums, watermelon, tomatoes, red apples, meat, radishes, seafood.

ORANGE FOODS > Need to make a decision? Want to face up to life's challenges? Ready for better health? Orange foods make people happier and help with decision making and to face problems. And wearing orange, even as an accessory, can make you communicate better.

Great orange foods: Oranges, mangoes, carrots, papaya, egg yolks, pumpkin, pepper, ginger.

YELLOW FOODS > Want to make new friends, be more popular and have a more positive outlook on life? Eat more yellow foods! They are known to give you an abundance of energy and enthusiasm, and it's the colour that feeds the brain and boosts the nervous system. Wearing yellow will also make you feel more cheerful.

Great yellow foods: Pineapple, bananas, grapefruits, melons, camomile tea, whole grains, honey, rice, nuts, lentils.

GREEN FOODS > Want more stability and balance in your life? Eating green foods gives you a feeling of calm, and also grounds you and brings more love into your life. Not to mention that they help you fight ageing and make you look younger! Wearing green can also aid with healing if you're not feeling too good.

Great green foods: Lemons, limes, lettuce, olive oil, milk, cabbage, broccoli, live yoghurt, cucumber, green beans.

BLUE FOODS > Not sleeping well? Feeling anxious or tense? Start eating more from this group. Blue foods help you clear your thoughts and let go of worries and fears so you can move on, and assist you to sleep well. Wearing blue is also soothing and relaxing.

Great blue foods: Blue plums, blueberries, wild mushrooms, prunes, blackberries, black soybeans, some white fresh fish, olives, cheese, garlic, seaweed.

PURPLE FOODS >

Want to be more spiritual, increase your intuition and be more creative? Add some purple foods to your diet, as they can help you get in tune with your body and your mind and become more sensitive. Wearing purple can also make you more intuitive and feel more uplifted – although wearing or eating too much can lead to spiritual burnout.

Great purple foods: Red grapes, eggplant, purple plums, purple cabbage, purple broccoli, Spanish onions, turnips, beetroot, mackerel.

AFFIRMATIONS FOR HEALTH > Visualisations and affirmations can help you achieve any goal, including health and happiness. Try some of these, or make up your own to lead you to your personal goals.

STEP 1 > Write out your affirmation on two pieces of yellow paper, so you can stick one to the fridge and one to the phone – this means you will see them constantly throughout the day. Try something like: "I am healthy and fit," "I am perfectly happy the way I am now," "I no longer crave coffee," "I love myself and am content with myself," "I will look fantastic," or "I will lose weight," whatever affirmation suits you best. Every time you walk past the fridge or see it by the phone, yell your affirmation aloud, then close your eyes and visualise yourself happy and healthy. You can also stick a photo of yourself in a happy moment on the bathroom mirror, to remind yourself of how wonderful your life is and will continue to be.

STEP 2 > If fitness or weight loss is your goal, start walking more, especially up hills as this is good for firming and toning your muscles as well as getting fit. As you walk chant: "Small bum! Trim tum!" It's amazing and almost hypnotic – and should bring a little chuckle to your lips as you walk. Wearing a jasper necklace can also help promote more effective weight loss.

STEP 3 > Do lots of fun activities and things you enjoy, and spend time with friends who inspire, uplift and encourage you. Celebrate every achievement, no matter how small. The more positive you feel about yourself the better, because it's all about attitude and truly wanting to feel better about yourself. You just have to visualise yourself where you want to be and you will get there.

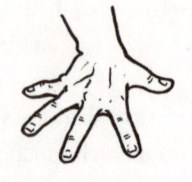

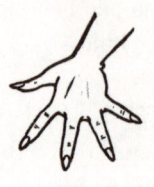

HAND GAMES > This hand game is a really fun way of seeing what's in store for you in the future. Sit at a table – make sure all the dishes are cleared off first! – put your hands in the air then slam them both down on the table. Notice how your left and right hands fall, and check out the following predictions to see what it means. This is a fun game to play with your friends as well.

Hands wide apart > You're feeling really restless and lots of change is coming.

Hands close together >	You're feeling insecure and not ready to take a risk at the moment.
Right hand stretched out >	There is travel and perhaps a change in residence or job ahead for you.
Left hand stretched out >	You're dwelling in what could have been or what is in the past – move on!
Fingers touching close together >	You're bottling up your emotions, which could lead to ill health in your future if care is not taken.
Fingers closed on right hand >	You're holding a secret in or are scared of being a failure.

HAND GAMES

Fingers closed on left hand >	Lots of mistakes have been made in the past.
Largest gap between ring and middle fingers >	A love affair, renewed passion in your existing relationship or a new lover is on the way.
Right hand fingers widely spaced >	Expect to have lots of fun with social activities and travel in the coming weeks.
Left hand fingers widely spaced >	Money worries and problems sleeping are foretold for you now.
Right hand pointed inwards >	Secretly you want to let your hair down and be more outgoing – a makeover is on the horizon.

HAND GAMES > 117

Left hand pointed inwards >	You're holding on to a secret.
Right little finger outstretched >	Passion is oozing! Place the "do not disturb" sign on your bedroom door!
Left little finger outstretched >	An ending to a relationship or friendship is indicated.
Right thumb outstretched >	A win or a successful outcome is likely in the near future.
Left thumb outstretched >	Fraud, deceit or a Judas figure looms large for you, so be extra careful!
Both hands hunched up >	You're ready for some excitement and action – and that's what's in store for you!

Right hand hunched up, left hand flat >	Financial opportunities will be offered to you within the next year. Strong career advancement and learning new skills is also indicated.
Left hand hunched up, right hand flat >	You need to take a risk. Be prepared for lots of opportunities both financially and personally and be patient.

HELLO!

HANDWRITING >

HANDWRITING ANALYSIS > Graphology is the art of assessing someone's character from their handwriting. It is an effective way of revealing their personality and behaviours, and can be used to predict the best career path, a suitable marriage partner, their financial future – it's even used in crime investigations. Take a peek at a friend's writing or look at your own, then consult the table on the following pages to see what it reveals.

WRITING STYLE >

Heavy pressure > Serious, committed and ambitious, can sometimes be a bit uptight. Excessively heavy pressure can betray a domineering control freak with a bad temper.

Light pressure > Sensitive and compassionate, but can lack stamina and the drive to succeed.

Right slant > Good communicator, friendly and optimistic.

Excessive right slant > Talkative, runs on nervous energy and thinks they are always right.

Left slant > Dwells in the past, doesn't like change and can be reserved emotionally.

Excessive left slant >	Can be manipulative, especially if the writing is large.
Small and delicate >	A logical, clear thinker, good communicator, but doesn't like to take risks.
Large > **Angled >**	Extrovert, outgoing, confident. Sharp points rather than a curved style indicate someone who is good in business and a perfectionist.
Threadlike >	Mentally alert, adaptable, clever, artistic, but can lack patience.
Wavy >	Skilful, passionate, resourceful and highly capable.

WORD SPACING >

Wide >	Can't stand restrictions or taking orders – they're crying out: "Give me space!"
Narrow >	An intrusive, smothering personality who needs to be with people.
Crowded >	Disorganised, messy and chaotic.

MARGINS >

Wide left >	Indicates someone with a need to move on and a fear of the past.
Narrow left >	Cautious and strong, will not be pushed into anything.
Left wider at top >	Very ambitious, ready to achieve a lot and reach their goals.
Left wider at bottom >	Energetic, good instincts, practical and impulsive.

Right widening to end of page >	This is the handwriting of an artificial person who may not be trustworthy.
Straight lines of text >	Reliable, orderly, responsible, can lack emotions if extreme.
Lines sloping upwards >	Optimistic, overambitious, excitable and restless.
Lines sloping downwards >	Can sometimes indicate depression and pessimism. The more extreme the line slopes down, the more serious the depressive state.

THE ENVELOPE >
How you address an envelope can reveal a lot about you.

Legible >	Considerate.
Illegible >	Careless and self-important.

Overstyled lettering >	Vain and pretentious.
Underlining >	Compulsive worrier.
Address in centre of envelope >	Clear thinker, good organiser, balanced.
Address at top >	Daydreamer, immature.
Address at bottom >	May reveal depression.
Extreme right, heavy pressure >	Impulsive, may have aggressive tendencies.

SIGNATURE >

Legible >	Honest, will honour commitments.
Completely illegible >	Vain, considers themselves superior.
Smaller first name, larger surname >	Early life traumas, can be domineering.

Larger first name >	Happy childhood memories, but can be childish.
Fine penmanship >	Respect for traditional values.
Artistic signature >	Putting on an act.
Full stop after signature >	Conventional attitudes.
Threadlike >	Signature of a manipulator – beware.
Larger than script >	Self-importance, desire to be recognised.
Smaller than script >	Modest. If extremely small it reveals low self-esteem.

UNDERSCORE >

Thick and long >   Ambitious, with an aggressive drive.
Normal pressure >   Self-confidant.
Crossed >   Money conscious.
Strong and rising >   Successful.

INK COLOUR >

Black >   Powerful.
Royal blue >   Feminine, loving, fun lover.
Dark blue >   Business like, no desire to pretend.
Pale blue >   Artistic.
Red >   Angry and aggressive.
Green >   Harmonious and a lover of wide open spaces.

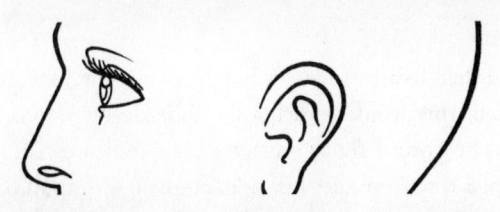

HEAD READING > Phrenology is the reading or assessing of a person's character by investigating and interpreting the bumps on their head. It was introduced in the 1790s by an Austrian physician, Dr Franz Gall, who came up with the theory that thinking affects the shape of the brain, and thus the shape of the skull, causing bumps that would be indicative of different areas of someone's personality. Basically if one area of the brain was overdeveloped it would grow bigger and create a bump in the skull. Alternatively if that area of thinking was underdeveloped it would be smaller, and result in an indent (the opposite of a bump) in the skull. Although not widely used today as a method of divination, it's still a fun exercise, and can reveal something of a person's character.

To do it, run your hands gently over your head, or a friend's. Consulting the map overleaf, make note of any areas where you have a significant lump, and also whether there are any places that seem to have a hollow or indent. According to Dr Gall, this would indicate an underdevelopment of that trait. The size of the bump or indent indicates the degree to which a person has this characteristic – a small bump at number 12 can indicate self-assurance and healthy pride, while a large lump can mean terrible arrogance.

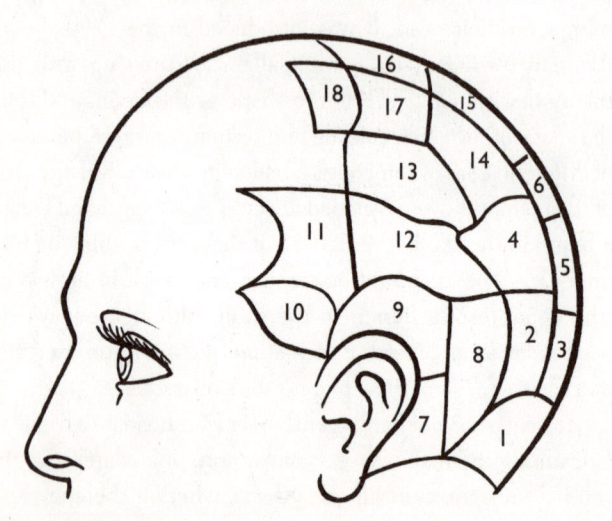

HEAD READING > 129

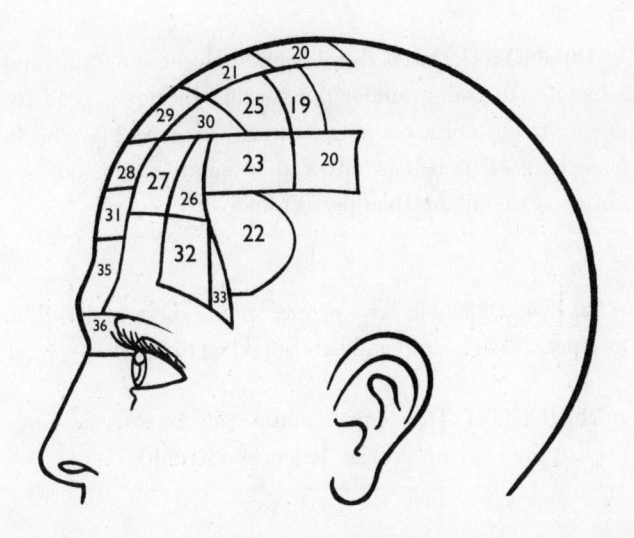

WHAT EACH AREA REPRESENTS >

> **1a) BUMP.** Controlling in relationships and can be a bit obsessive – this is doubly intensified if there is a bump in this position on either side of the head. Watch out for this if you find it in a new partner!

> **1b) INDENT.** Need desperately to have a partner and affection. If leading under the ear, it indicates a need for commitment and a life-long partner. These people tend to have long relationships rather than short affairs, but are always searching for their perfect mate.

> **2a) BUMP.** Need to have people around them in their life, love pets and children and hate spending time alone.

> **2b) INDENT.** They enjoy solitude and in extreme cases neglect their friends and are loners and hermits.

> **3a) BUMP.** Very patriotic – and the bigger the bump, the more fervent the patriotism (some would say racism) and sense of traditional values.

> **3b) INDENT.** Curious and open minded, and feel a desire to explore other nationalities and cultures.

> **4a) BUMP.** Need variety in life, often restless, get bored easily, crave action, excitement and change.

> **4b) INDENT.** Can be lacking in personality and be considered by some to be a little boring. Take forever to tell a story, and talk about themselves a lot.

5a) BUMP. Quick-witted, fiery type, excitable and feisty.

5b) INDENT. Timid, reserved, sometimes cowardly.

> **6a) BUMP.** A ruthless, unforgiving revenge seeker! If really large and noticeable it is known as the "criminal's bump". Take care if you're in a relationship with a person with this lump.

> **6b) INDENT.** An underdeveloped area here is a good thing, and indicates a peace seeker.

> **7a) BUMP.** This is about a person's appetite. A small bump indicates a healthy appetite and enjoyment of food and wine, but a large bump reveals a greedy glutton who overindulges in all things.

> **7b) INDENT.** Underdevelopment here can reveal a picky eater who must take care to eat well and not diet or exercise obsessively.

> **8a) BUMP.** Someone who is wasteful, buys things without needing them and throws out a lot of good things, such as new, unworn clothes with the tags still attached.

> **8b) INDENT.** A clutter bug who won't throw anything out and hordes things for a rainy day, even when they are no longer useful.

> **9a) BUMP.** Clever and quick thinking, but the bigger the bump, the more cunning – a real-life Judas or smiling assassin.

> **9b) INDENT.** Open and honest, but the more underdeveloped the more gullible the person.

> **10a) BUMP.** This is a prudish type who has a fear of the unknown and is quite timid.

> **10b) INDENT.** A person who is careless, reckless and impulsive.

> **11a) BUMP.** Love to be admired, extremely sensitive, and the bigger the bump, the more vain and conceited the person.

> **11b) INDENT.** Unconcerned with their appearance or looking after themselves, which in its extreme form can manifest in bad hygiene, unkempt hair and dirty clothes.

> **12a) BUMP.** A small bump indicates healthy pride and self-respect, but a larger one reveals extreme pride and arrogance.

> **12b) INDENT.** A lack of self-pride, self-respect and personal appreciation.

> **13a) BUMP.** This person finds it easy to make decisions, which in an extreme state can lead to hasty choices that aren't thought through properly.

> **13b) INDENT.** Take forever to make decisions, which means they miss out on opportunities.

> **14a) BUMP.** Sexual, passionate, and confident in the bedroom.

> **14b) INDENT.** Shy sexually, which in its extreme case can indicate serious inhibitions.

> **15a) BUMP.** Exaggerator, makes too many promises, optimistic, very positive.

> **15b) INDENT.** Pessimist, always seeing gloom and doom and worry, negative.

> **16a) BUMP.** Very intuitive and potentially very psychic.

> **16b) INDENT.** Sceptical and can be lacking in faith of any kind.

> **17a) BUMP.** Makes sacrifices for others, and wants to make the world a better place.

> **17b) INDENT.** Very selfish, and thinks only: "Me! Me! Me!"

> **18a) BUMP.** Intelligent.

> **18b) INDENT.** Average intelligence.

> **19a) BUMP.** Has high endurance and good staying power in the bedroom, at work, in sport etc.

> **19b) INDENT.** Lacks vitality and can be lazy.

> **20a) BUMP.** Bright, vital, fun loving and a good communicator, in extremes it can indicate a total extrovert or exhibitionist.

> **20b) INDENT.** Introverted and shy.

> **21a) BUMP.** Material security is of the utmost importance.

> **21b) INDENT.** A risk taker and gambler.

> **22a) BUMP.** Has a good sense of humour if not too excessive, but if the bump is large it can indicate a cruel edge, someone who ridicules others for their misfortune and laughs at people's mistakes.

> **22b) INDENT.** Not much of a sense of humour.

> **23a) BUMP.** Curious, but can also reveal an arrogance and an attitude that they are always right.

> **23b) INDENT.** Has a thirst for knowledge and loves to study and learn.

> **24a) BUMP.** Good memory for people, shapes, forms, spelling etc.

> **24b) INDENT.** Poor memory for faces, names, shapes etc.

> **25a) BUMP.** Ability to judge sizes, measurements and distances accurately.

> **25b) INDENT.** Has a strange sense of proportion and seldom judges correctly.

> **26a) BUMP.** Has good balance and feels comfortable up high, so would make an excellent sailor, pilot, traveller or astronaut and a great athlete.

> **26b) INDENT.** Has trouble with balance.

> **27a) BUMP.** Artistic and creative, with an understanding of colour and shading. Loves colourful homes and clothing and would work well in design or art.

> **27b) INDENT.** No appreciation for colour, prefers neutral tones and pale, colourless things.

> **28a) BUMP.** Efficient and organised, loves structure and definition and hates chaos.

> **28b) INDENT.** Messy, chaotic and careless, is happy to work in a disorganised office.

> **29a) BUMP.** Very logical, excellent at maths and calculating numbers.

> **29b) INDENT.** Has trouble calculating numbers.

> **30a) BUMP.** Has a great sense of direction and can find their way around.

> **30b) INDENT.** No sense of direction, gets lost easily.

> **31a) BUMP.** Can remember jokes and stories and is always recounting lengthy tales.

> **31b) INDENT.** Indicates forgetfulness, can't remember events or the punchline of jokes.

> **32a) BUMP.** Great musical timing and rhythm, and is punctual and good at remembering dates.

> **32b) INDENT.** A lack of musical talent and difficulty with timing.

> **33a) BUMP.** A born entertainer with a good singing voice, dancing ability and acting skills.

> **33b) INDENT.** Can't carry a tune or stand up and act naturally in front of a crowd – they are more confident behind the scenes and feel more comfortable there.

> **34a) BUMP.** Great talker, good salesman – has the gift of the gab and would make an excellent politician.

> **34b) INDENT.** Finds it hard to get ideas across and flow with conversations, but excels as someone's right-hand man.

> **35a) BUMP.** A brilliant ideas person who can be a genius.

> **35b) INDENT.** Comes up with ideas, but isn't very practical.

> **36a) BUMP.** Interested in people, but can be a stickybeak, gossip, and in extreme cases a backstabber.

> **36b) INDENT.** Keeps to themselves and doesn't like to interfere, but can be very secretive too.

I CHING MADE EASY > The I Ching, or Book of Changes, is an ancient Chinese oracle, a philosophical text that has been consulted by those seeking wisdom for the past 4000 years. It is based on patterns, or hexagrams, that are constructed by the throwing of several coins, then interpreted using the Book, which provides answers as well as advice on how best to incorporate the results into your life. It is a complex and in depth oracle that can give much insight and guidance into the situations, obstacles and choices you face. For a full reading you should buy a translation of the complete I Ching, but I have come up with a simplified version so that you can get a feel for it and start to experience the wonder that infuses this ancient form of divination.

Turn the page, close your eyes and, as you are asking your question, gently throw an I Ching coin (or a Chinese coin) on to the page and see which number it lands on. Alternatively you can close your eyes, spin the book around then see which number your finger (or a pin) is drawn to. You can even put the numbers on to pieces of paper, put them in a small bag then draw one out when you need some guidance or the answer to a question.

144 < I CHING MADE EASY

4 Meng	33 Tun	47 K'un	5 Hsu
48 Ching	54 Kuei mei	60 Chieh	16 Yu
23 Po	31 Hsien	1 Ch'ien	14 Ta yu
42 I	56 Lu	40 Hsieh	28 Ta kuo
58 Tui	2 K'un	37 Chia den	50 Ting
18 Ku	52 Ken	32 Heng	19 Lin
35 Chin	61 Chung fu	3 Chun	21 Shih ho
64 Wei chi	15 Ch'ien	43 Kuai	41 Sun

53 Chien	38 K'uei	24 Fu	63 Chi chi
13 T'ung jen	6 Sung	34 Ta chuang	46 Sheng
36 Ming I	26 Ta ch'u	51 Chen	20 Kuan
17 Sui	44 Kou	7 Shih	57 Sun
25 Wu wang	62 Hsiao kuo	22 Pi	12 P'i
8 Pi	59 Huan	11 T'ai	27 I
55 Feng	9 Hsiao ch'u	39 Chien	29 K'an
10 Lu	49 Ko	45 Ts'ui	30 Li

1. CH'IEN >
Success from creativity.
Difficulties will be easily overcome, you'll start something new and exciting and be more creative.

2. K'UN >
Receptivity.
There are obstacles and many challenges to face, but success is more than likely.

3. CHUN >
Difficulty at the beginning.
Don't start anything new at present as it's a difficult time, but you will soon lay the foundation for the success that will come in the future.

4. MENG >
Immaturity.
Don't be too critical of younger or less experienced people, instead encourage them and give positive advice when asked.

5. HSU >

Waiting.
Travel sets the course for success at this time – your future is manifesting now, and your life is taking new roads or directions.

6. SUNG >

Conflict.
Situations can usually be resolved if they are confronted wisely, but if you are struggling to overcome a problem, give up and let it go.

7. SHIH >

The army.
There are dangerous tasks ahead, so rely on expert opinions, get advice from those who know and tread very lightly at this time.

8. PI >

Unity.
Cooperation will bring progress, and good organisational help will come from someone in authority. Be grateful for this and accept the assistance gracefully.

9. HSIAO CH'U > The lesser nourisher.

Take your time – you are going to see a lot of progress in the near future, but for now remember that slow and steady wins the race. Be patient, and kind to others in need.

10. LU > Treading carefully.

Present situations are becoming difficult, but if you are cautious you will succeed. Watch out for affairs of the heart that could cause future problems.

11. T'AI > Peace.

This is a time of harmony and good fortune, where you will discover your inner strength and learn new skills.

12. P'I > Stagnation.

Disharmony and weakness surround you now, and are obstacles to reaching your goals.

13. T'UNG JEN > Universal brotherhood.

You will feel great fellowship with lovers and friends. Accept the situation for what it is and do not complain about anything now.

14. TA YU > Many possessions.

There is cultural achievement, huge success and victory, and a big reunion and celebration is near.

15. CH'IEN > Modesty.

Do not boast about material success, and help out someone in need for speedy spiritual growth.

16 YU > Enthusiasm.

Proceed if you feel confident you are on the right track, keep an even temper and don't neglect your loved ones.

17. SUI >

Following.
Be cautious of ulterior motives, be assertive and do what you want to do – don't hold back as you have a fire in your belly and are ready for action. And don't bottle anything up inside or you'll explode!

18. KU >

Decay.
There is turmoil now and ruined endings, but work on what has been destroyed – out of all the chaos will come new directions and the sun will shine again on your life.

19. LIN >

Approach.
You are ready to move on in an area of your life, and will gain a lot of wise advice from an older, more experienced person. An offer is also likely.

I CHING MADE EASY > 151

20. KUAN > **Contemplation.**
Take a hard look at your life and your goals, hopes and wishes, and ask yourself if it is still what you really want and whether it's worth pursuing.

21. SHIH HO > **Gnawing away.**
You will have legal or official successes, and while there may be separations, just remember you are not to blame.

22. PI > **Grace.**
Watch and learn from what's happening around you, because good luck is close by.

23. PO > **Separating.**
Get rid of all the clutter and baggage that is currently stopping you from reaching your goals.

24. FU > Returns.
Selfless giving, self-sacrifice and kindness to others is what is needed right now, and charitable work is ideal.

25. WU WANG > The unexpected.
Expect the unexpected, stick to your principles and do not give in to temptations.

26. TA CH'U > The great nourisher.
It's an excellent time for travel and fun times with friends. Your aura is electric and you'll be kicking huge goals personally and professionally.

27. I > Sustenance.
Consistent efforts will bring home the bacon, so hang in there, stay positive and learn from past mistakes.

I CHING MADE EASY > 153

28. TA KUO > **Excess.**
Watch out for overindulgence in rich foods and alcohol and too much overspending. Stick to a budget and practise moderation.

29. K'AN > **The abyss.**
Danger and deception surrounds you, so be aware of people and places and be careful of who you trust.

30. LI > **Fire.**
New directions are unfolding, and helping those less fortunate will be linked to success and luck financially or personally. You have an abundance of energy, but use your power wisely.

31. HSIEN > **Influence.**
Attraction, passion and commitments are ideal now for lovers and will bring good luck.

32. HENG > Duration.
Perseverance will pay off and you'll see results sooner than you thought, but your patience is being tested.

33. TUN > Retreat.
Pay attention to details and the immediate future – but do not make too many long-term plans or be sidetracked from the present.

34. TA CHUANG > The power of the great.
Do not be a fence sitter – this is the time to take a risk and follow new directions or plans.

35. CHIN > Progress.
Rewards are coming thick and fast, with self-pride and achievements, and a woman will bring luck or a proposal.

36. MING I >	**Darkening of the light.** Stop being selfish and instead think of others. Also keep your future plans close to your chest, as jealousy surrounds you now.
37. CHIA DEN >	**The family.** Family happiness is of the utmost importance now, so give them more of your time and make them your number one priority.
38. K'UEI >	**Opposition.** Slight setbacks now will only make you more determined and test your strength. Pleasant times with those you hold close to your heart are foretold.
39. CHIEN >	**Trouble.** Difficulty, temptations and possible danger are close by. Don't lend money or take

	risks, and wait for good advice from someone honest.
40. HSIEH >	**Release.** It's time to reassess your priorities and let go of what is stressing you or has no future.
41. SUN >	**Reduction.** A loss now will bring success in the long term. Avoid personal commitments at present.
42. I >	**Gain.** Past rejections will now come to fruition, and the rewards will flow thick and fast. Communication is also excellent, and a win is likely.
43. KUAI >	**Breakthrough.** Problems will finally be resolved, and a financial change for the better will occur,

but only trust those you are 100 per cent sure about.

44. KOU >

Contact.
Lots of business and social contact will take place – it's an excellent time for meeting new connections, and the time is ripe for changing your home or job or going travelling.

45. TS'UI >

Gathering.
There will be reunions and the end of conflicts, with successful communication a plus, but a sacrifice is needed.

46. SHENG >

Promotion.
You'll be moving up the ladder financially and have good luck personally – just believe in yourself and you'll see a wish come true!

47. K'UN > Exhaustion.
Take time out to smell the roses and relax, or you risk burnout. Start some gentle exercise and eat well, and take a holiday or at least some time out to have fun.

48. CHING > The well.
Be assertive and make the most of the opportunities presented to you now. Be bold and daring and speak out for what you want.

49. KO > Revolution.
Home renovations or reinventing yourself are likely and probably necessary. Be flexible and make the necessary changes to get yourself out of the rut you've been in.

50. TING > Sacrificial urn.
Helping someone less fortunate than yourself will make you feel good, and encourage you to reassess your priorities and make positive changes.

51. CHEN > Thunder.
Power surrounds you in the months ahead, but it's important to use it wisely – helping others also creates a good vibe for your own personal growth.

52. KEN > Keeping still.
Your spiritual growth is enormous now, and your intuition will improve. Relax, meditate and listen to your inner voice and the messages and guidance from above. You have been missing the signs.

53. CHIEN >

Gradual progress.
Marriage success is indicated, with constant change, movement and travel shown.

54. KUEI MEI >

The marrying maiden.
This is an unfortunate omen for a woman. Beware of marriage and proposals at this time, and see people for what they really are. Is this love or lust?

55. FENG >

Abundance.
This abundance could be good news or bad news depending on what efforts you have put in in the past, and whether you have acted with integrity or not. Those who have been misers will have a troubled week, as past generosities are rewarded now.

56. LU >	**The traveller.** Travel is likely now, but be careful of accidents or being blamed for someone else's mistakes. If you don't go anywhere, there will be long distance communication.
57. SUN >	**Willing submission.** Be flexible and adaptable, as this is a time when carefully made plans will be thrown out the window. You will receive good advice from a powerful man in your favour.
58. TUI >	**Joy.** Success is sweet, and you will have happiness in abundance. Enjoy this blissful time.
59. HUAN >	**Dispersing.** This is a time favourable to travel, and long distance communication will bring good news – just be honest about your mistakes.

60. CHIEH >

Limitations.
If you're feeling anxious or depressed, change your life's course right now, and make the necessary moves to a happier future.

61. CHUNG FU >

Inner truth.
Courage and persistence will bring success, and a new-found confidence will see you a winner in all stakes.

62. HSIAO KUO >

The power of the small.
Small successes are likely right now, and bigger ones are on the way.

63. CHI CHI >

After completion.
Good fortune abounds right now, but be careful of losses. Important decisions also need to be made.

64. WEI CHI > Before completion.

You're nearly halfway there. Obstacles and hiccups will test your strength, but stay strong and focused and you'll make it.

MOLE PREDICTIONS > Interpreting moles, known as moleoscopy, is a form of divination where meaning is given to the shape and position of moles on the body. The location of a mole is said to reveal a lot about what's inside a person and what they are really like. Bigger and darker moles and multiple moles have more significance than smaller, lighter and less noticeable ones. In ancient times much store was placed in this method, and people were judged harshly if they had a big mole on certain parts of their bodies, but today it is more of a fun exercise than a serious consideration of a person's character. *Note:* It's important to be especially careful to cover moles from the sun. If moles get larger or change shape or colour it could indicate skin cancer, so get them checked out.

MOLE PREDICTIONS

Forehead > If located on the right side you are very lucky, and recognition, honour, fame and great wealth could be yours. If it is on the left side however life will be a bit of a struggle and you will have to work hard for success.

Eyebrows > If you have a mole between your brows it indicates that you are excitable, active and a deep thinker. The larger it is though the more selfish you can be, and you need to keep your ego in check.

Eyes or close to > This indicates honesty and forthrightness, but can also mean low self-esteem and a need for lots of attention and love. Be careful who you choose as your friends and lovers.

Nose > A mole on your nose indicates that you are sincere and loyal and an excellent marriage or business partner. You can also achieve a lot of wealth no matter what circumstances life brings you.

Ears > You can be reckless and spontaneous, and need to put in more effort to achieve things. Success will not be handed to you on a plate – although if you really work at it and follow your dreams you could find fame.

Cheeks > You are serious, spiritual and always searching for life's purpose. You're not interested in superficial relationships or wealth – you'd rather find inner peace and purpose.

Lips or close to > You are never satisfied, always searching for perfection within yourself and very self-critical. You're always looking for a better way of living, and the more towards the left the mole is, the more you dwell in the past and yearn for greener pastures.

Chin > You love challenges and none are too big to face – you strive for success and will achieve a lot through your conscientious and commonsense approach to life.

Neck > You are sincere, shy, gentle and classy, and quite selective with your friends and lovers. You will have ups and downs in your life, but you will get through them all and come out on top.

Shoulders > You excel in sports. A mole on your left shoulder can reveal a tendency to be easily satisfied, which can lead to happiness, while one on the right shoulder indicates you are careful, loyal yet a little restless.

Arms >

You are happy and have a good sense of humour and counselling skills. If it is on the left arm you are also polite, serious and determined, while if it's on the right arm you will tend to have a harder younger life but be happy and content later.

Chest >

You are family orientated, with a love of children and a passionate demeanour with your partner, but you can struggle with your finances and tend to be a little lazy.

Breasts >

A mole on the right breast can mean you're good in relationships but can sometimes be a bit of a troublemaker and argumentative, while one on the left reveals you are active, health conscious and interested in outdoor exercise.

Nipples >	You could have a tendency to be a little fickle, and drawn to high social status.
Stomach >	You love a good time, good food and good friends, but can sometimes be a little self-indulgent. You may also have a weakness for gambling, and be a tad impatient.
Bottom >	A mole on your buttocks indicates that you are highly sexed yet lacking in ambition.
Legs >	You will experience many changes in life and perhaps even live in a foreign country. You are adaptable to change and always moving and changing jobs. On the left leg it can indicate a bad temper and possible laziness, on the right leg it reveals that you are energetic but may run from commitments.

Knees >

A mole on the left knee indicates good business sense, spontaneity and possible problems with your knees, such as arthritis or injuries. A mole on the right knee reveals friendliness and a love of travel and the outdoors.

Feet >

You need to feel secure, and don't really like taking big risks. You're thoughtful, willing to share, practical and have a good sense of humour.

NUMEROLOGY > Numerology, also known as numeromancy or arithomancy, is the science of numbers. As a form of divination it is used by interpreting the numbers of your birth date or even your name. The roots of numerology reach back to mathematician and philosopher Pythagoras, who believed that numbers had a vibration that affects us, and that everything could be expressed in numbers. The easiest way to use numerology is to calculate the number of your birth date and find out what is in store for you this year. Simply add the date and month of your birth together, disregarding the year in which you were born. Then add 9 to find out your fortune for 2007 (2+0+0+7=9), or 1 for 2008 (2+0+0+8=10, reduced to 1+0=1), or 2 for 2009 (2+0+0+9=11, reduced to 1+1=2) and so on.

To find out about the year 2007 for someone born on May 12, add 5 (for May), 3 (for the 12th – 1+2), and 9 for the year. Their fortune for the year 2007 would thus be 5+3+9=17, then 1+7=8, so they would read the meaning for the number eight below. The cycle for each year will start for you from your birthday, so this person would be an eight from May 12, 2007 to May 11, 2008.

ONE > This is a year for fresh starts, and a time to be bold and daring. Take risks, speak up for what you believe in and want and don't sit on the fence, because opportunities are all around you, as are soulmate connections of either new friends or lovers. Be prepared for plenty of change and a better way of life opening up for you. It's a rebirth after last year's chaos and endings, and is an excellent time to buy property, start a business or begin a new romance. In this dynamic year you will be more determined and have the courage needed to reach your goals. It is a time to take charge of your life and lead it to where you want to go. It's a great time to reinvent yourself, give yourself a makeover and get fit and healthy, as willpower is at a peak for you this year.

TWO > This is a slow year in which harmony is of the utmost importance. You must take care of your health, as there will be some emotional upheavals either with yourself or close family members. There will be endings, losses or stressful situations to deal with too, and you will also be heavily in demand with family concerns. This is a period when many will look at how much love they have in their life – or how little – and do something about it. As a result singles could make a lasting commitment, and it's an ideal time to marry or form long-lasting relationships and friendships. Many others will separate and move on. It is a time that is enormously spiritual, your intuition will be extremely high, and many will experience an awakening of some kind. Health issues may crop up, and it is important to eat correctly, get plenty of exercise and take good care of yourself so more serious health problems don't occur. Patience will be needed to see this year through.

THREE > Socially you'll be having a ball this year. It's an excellent time for communication and climbing the career or financial ladder, with luck in increasing your wealth. You could find you are in the right place at the right time to meet the right connections, personally or business-wise. Stay alert to the outstanding opportunities that the year will bring. Reunions loom large, as do lots of family celebrations, marriages and long distance communication. There will be new friendships forming with people from all walks of life – you are more charismatic and popular this year than usual. Love is set to sizzle, and travel is also highly likely. It is a time of change to – a new career, job, address or partner is more than likely to materialise. This year is a time to face up to your challenges and problems rather than sweeping things under the carpet, so you can grow and move on. It's a highly creative time, and those working in the entertainment or writing fields could be in the limelight, as fame is not uncommon now. Expansion and personal growth is what this year is all about, so reach for the stars.

FOUR > This is the year you will lay your foundations for the rest of your life, like a builder laying his slab. You will make long-term plans and feel security conscious, so it is very important to have positive people around you, as negative types will zap your confidence and self-esteem. Restrictions around finances could cause frustrations and health concerns, as some could find themselves becoming workaholics, so it is important to take time out to rest and relax. If you stay focused on your goals and are not afraid of hard work you will be dumbfounded by what you will achieve this year, and really find a lot more security in your life financially. Concerning relationships, singles could find themselves attracted to the wrong types and mistake love for lust, so be extra careful. Separations can occur in existing relationships, and it is important to see people for what they are and beware of deception. Passionate affairs are more common in this cycle than most, so avoid temptation. More divorces also take place in this year than any other, and the need for security leads to many singles getting mixed up in relationships they should not be in just for the sake of having someone in their life. Over all however a lot can be achieved.

It is an excellent time to find success and increase your collateral with real estate or investments. You will be amazed by what you achieve if you stay positive and confident.

FIVE > This year can make a person feel like they have ants in their pants! The need to run away from problems, to travel and change your life is what this year is all about. It's a turning point, and many career opportunities will present themselves, with progress and strong advancement on the work front also likely. Lots of challenges and added responsibilities will make this year very busy. You may feel the need to change your appearance, travel overseas or see your own country – lots of movement is likely in all different ways. A change of residence will definitely be on the cards for many, and singles will have a lot of fun dating and meeting lots of new friends. There will also be overseas connections and helpful people both personally and professionally. In relationships you will want to run away from clinging vines and commitments, as you won't want restrictions, but rather need to be free to chase your rainbows and do what you want. Be careful not to be too impulsive or act recklessly though. The year will be action packed and you will feel like a video on fast forward. It's full steam ahead, but push the pause button occasionally. Basically this is an action year, and it's also known as the bachelor year. Love is in the air big time.

SIX > These 12 months will be extremely busy for you and your family. You will be heavily in demand, and this could lead to a build up of resentment as there will be periods when it seems that there is no time for your own needs. However you will feel so rewarded by the end of the year and realise how truly loved you are. This year many will decide to become involved in the community and make their mark. It's also an excellent time to fall in love, as your aura will have that extra sparkle that attracts the right type of partner into your life – more marriages take place in this numerical vibration than any other. Singles also generally find a beautiful long-lasting commitment. Lots of babies are born too, as the emphasis is on close personal relationships and new family members through births and marriages. This year will see all age groups make lasting friendships, great new business connections and further their careers and finances. You will want to be around those you hold special in your heart, and want to feel more settled than at any other time. Those in the teaching, counselling and community-based fields can expect to be busier than ever and jump hugely towards their goals.

SEVEN > This year it's very important to get rid of all the clutter in your life – this means frustrating relationships, friendships, business deals that have gone sour and other emotional baggage. It's a time that is all about spiritual growth, and the key to success is to rise above your own problems by getting involved in other people's, helping those in need or less fortunate than yourself. Basically this is your time to give. Those who have a hard time at that will find the year challenging. There will be many obstacles to overcome, but this will only test where your strengths lie and further you spiritually. Most will have psychic experiences of some kind, and your intuition will be at its peak. Many people will question their faith and beliefs, and there can be serious losses or endings in relationships. The key is to hang in there, rise to the challenge and take time out away from the hustle and bustle – wide open spaces will appeal to you. It will be a difficult year, but your whole life will change for the better if you're willing to put in the effort. This is also an excellent time to specialise in a new career, study or take up hobbies.

EIGHT > This is a cracker year for those who have put in the effort and worked hard. You will have an added strength to your aura that will see you march forward in leaps and bounds. This is a time to make major purchases, move up the career ladder and zoom ahead in business. And if you find the necessary balance in your personal and business lives and don't neglect relationships, you will have a successful love life. The number eight is all about power, and what you do with the power given is very important. Those who are selfish and think only of themselves could find that they lose everything. It's a great time for accumulating more wealth – but it's also a time that many go bankrupt due to neglect and greed. But for most people, this year will see your life improve greatly, and you will kick many goals and make your mark. Many powerful marriages occur now, as well as new business ventures.

NINE > A thirst for knowledge and greater understanding is what this year is all about. There will be a lot of endings in your life, and the presence of dramas around relationships. It is a time to let go of anything that has no more use to you so that you can go into next year's 1 cycle fresh and free of baggage. Those who cling to possessions, people and past situations will not be able to move forward. This is the time to let go of all baggage – it's now or never. Many relationships will end, and although not impossible, this is a tough year for singles to find a long-lasting relationship, as it is more about endings. However this means that troublesome relationships will disappear or become stronger, so there is good in everything. This year is also about compassion and helping people, and you will feel the need to go out and do charitable work, learn a new skill or advance your career. There will be many rewards on the financial and career front, and a change in residence is more than likely. Long distance communication and new friendships with people born overseas will also occur, and there will be lots of travel, reunions and property purchases. You will feel more compassionate towards those who suffer in the world and want to do something about this. Those who deserve it will be rewarded, and doctors, healers and counsellors will see their practices become busier than ever. Your intuition will be extremely high, so go with your gut feelings. Animals will play a big role for many, and you will receive special guidance towards your life's purpose this year.

OMENS & SUPERSTITIONS > Fortune telling and divination have had a lot of superstitions attached to them over the centuries. Some of them are true, and really do work, but others may be more old wives tale than reality. Try them out and decide for yourself!

Amber beads >	Worn around the neck, amber beads can prevent a cold and illness.
Ants >	The appearance of lots of ants around the home foretells rain.

Baby predictions >	Using a pendulum made from a wedding ring threaded on a piece of hair, cotton or string, swing it above the pregnant woman's stomach. If the ring swings in circles it's a girl, if it swings straight it's a boy.
Beds >	Buy a new mattress when you meet a new partner or are going to marry, as a bed carries some of the energy of past relationships.
Bees >	If a bee lands on you it is very good luck, and if one enters your home you will have great fortune all year.
Birds >	Willy wagtails seen often around your home are messengers from angels and deceased loved ones. And many birds in flight indicates that rain is coming.

OMENS & SUPERSTITIONS

Boat >   A sailing boat filled with gold nuggets and displayed in the home brings prosperity.

Bridge >   Don't say goodbye to anyone on a bridge, as you will never see them again.

Butterflies >   If you see a white butterfly you will have happiness and good luck all year, and if you see three coloured butterflies together you will have a wish granted.

Candles >   A pink or red candle is great for love. To win a court case, burn a green one, and to be more popular use yellow or orange. To attract wealth light a red, purple or orange candle.

Cat >   If a black cat is walking towards you, you will be lucky soon, but if it is running away you will suffer a loss in wealth or a relationship.

Chinese I Ching coins >	To increase wealth, tie three to your key ring with a red ribbon. To fall pregnant, pin six small ones to the right side of your bed, tied with red ribbon. Place some in the till and on your invoice books and computer for business success. Put three around the phone for important calls to come, and attach some to the front door to bring in good luck and sell a property.
Chinese money cats >	These are great in the front door of a shop to attract business.
Crickets >	If a cricket enters your home you will be successful.
Crystal ball >	Place a small crystal ball to the left of your desk for career advancement.

Dragon >	A dragon placed on the right side of your desk makes you wealthy and successful, and placed inside the home facing the door it attracts household prosperity.
Ears >	If you place your little finger inside your ear and it turns around easily you're generous, if it's a tight fit then you're selfish and tight with money.
Electrical equipment >	Try to limit TVs, stereos etc in the bedroom as they disrupt the flow of energy. Move them out or cover them with a sheet at night.
Fish >	Fish ornaments and pictures throughout the home are lucky.

Four leaf clover >	If you find one of these it is very lucky for finances – make a wish now!
Friday the 13th >	Don't cut your hair or start a new relationship on this day as it will bring bad luck.
Frogs >	A frog in the home is very lucky and good news will follow. Placing a frog statue facing the front door or in the garden will bring money opportunities.
Hand itch >	If it's the left hand it means you'll be paying money out, if it's the right you're winning.
Herb garden >	Planting a herb garden or fruit trees improves the health of the household.
Horseshoe >	One of these hung above the doorway brings very good luck. And if a bride wears

	one on her wedding day it should be a successful union.
Ladders >	Don't walk under a ladder or you will suffer ill health and bad luck.
Ladybugs >	If a ladybug lands on you, romance is coming soon or your current relationship will remain passionate.
Laughing Buddhas >	One of these displayed in the home creates great happiness.
Mirrors >	Placing a small round mirror under the mattress will attract a potential husband or wife to a single person. And breaking one is said to bring seven years of bad luck.

OMENS & SUPERSTITIONS > 189

Onions > Make a wish while burning onion skins in the flames of a fire.

Oranges > Keeping a big bowl of oranges in the kitchen is extremely lucky for singles to attract a prosperous partner.

Pebbles > Make some lucky stones by gluing together nine river stones and spraying them gold, and place in the garden near the front door for outstanding wealth and career success.

Photos > Placing loving pictures in the far right corner of your lounge room or bedroom brings more love and harmony into your life.

Pink sheets > Make the bed with these for extra passion.

Property >	If you're trying to sell a property, write the word "sold" across a picture of it, and place yellow flowers around the home.
Shoes >	Never place shoes on the table as this is extremely unlucky. If you've had a stressful day leave your shoes outside as it keeps the worries out of the home so you have time to relax. But don't clutter your front door with shoes – keep it clear for positive energies to flow through.
Spider >	If a spider is weaving a web in the morning it's good luck, if it's the afternoon you will travel soon. If one lands on you money wins and luck are likely, and if it weaves a web in a doorway a visitor will arrive soon.

GOOD LUCK OMENS >
> A wishbone from a chicken.
> Looking at the new moon over your right shoulder.
> Picking up a five cent piece.
> Bats flying after sunset.
> A rabbit's foot.
> Seeing a bluebird.
> A sprig of white heather.
> Spilling your drink when proposing a toast.

BAD LUCK OMENS >
> Seeing an owl during the day.
> Putting an umbrella up inside.
> Seeing a black cat walk under a ladder.
> Killing a spider.
> An itchy nose.
> Dropping a pair of scissors.
> Bringing a sprig of wattle inside the house.
> Breaking your glass when proposing a toast.

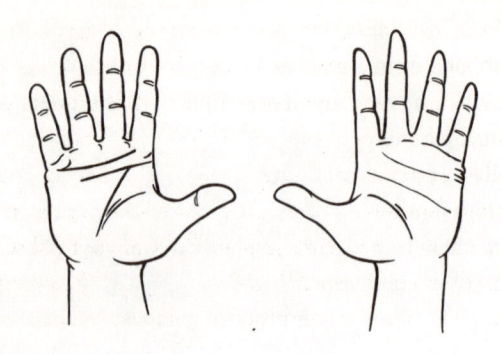

PALMISTRY > This is the reading of a person's future by interpr-eting the lines and marks on their hands. It is also known as chirognomy, chirology or chiromancy, from the Greek word "cheir", meaning hand, and has been used throughout time and across cultures, including ancient Greece and Egypt. It later became popular with the gypsies of Europe, and it is those associations that live on in modern folklore.

The beginning point to reading the future in a palm is to look at both hands. The left hand is said to indicate the potential you were born with, and the future you were destined to have, while the right reveals your personality and nature now, and what the future may hold. (If you are left-handed this is reversed.) Remember though that a person's future can change – and so can the marks on their hands – over time, through choices they make and the paths they take. You can take a picture or photocopy of your palm, then look at it again in 12 months, and you will see the changes it has undergone, and be able to see a picture of your life then and how it is now.

In palmistry there are many different things that can reveal your past and your future, from every marking and line on your palms to the basic shape of your hands, the patterns on finger tips, the length and width of bumps and mounds – all these things hold incredibly valuable information about you. Importantly no one's palm is the same as anyone else's, each one is unique.

To begin a reading, decide which kind of hand you have. Most people have one of four types of hands – earth, air, fire or water - which are described on the following pages.

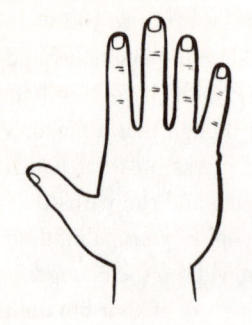

AN EARTH HAND > is square shaped, with thickish short fingers and usually a few very deep lines. People with this hand type are very security conscious and hardworking, and don't like too much change to routine or traditions.

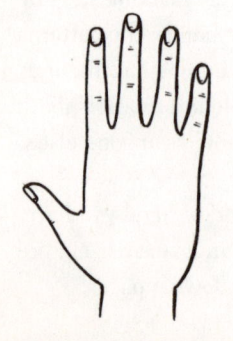

AN AIR HAND > is square shaped but with long fingers, and lines are not as deep as with earth hands. Mentally these people are very alert, restless types with sharp minds, who become bored easily.

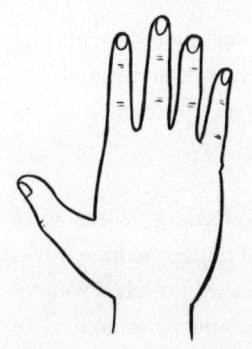

A FIRE HAND > has a longer palm than the fingers. People with these hands are usually very energetic and expressive types with dynamic personalities. They are excellent communicators, showy, colourful and fun loving.

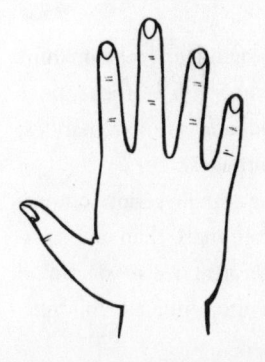

A WATER HAND > has both a long palm and long fingers. These people are very sensitive and gentle, stress easily, are artistic and creative and prone to daydreaming.

LOVE > The most common question palm readers are asked is about love and children, so here is some guidance for interpreting the palm and its lines on this topic.

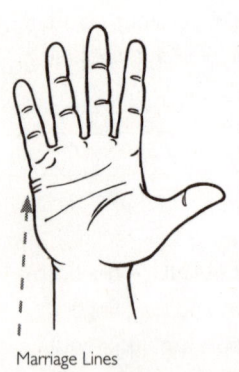

MARRIAGE LINES > These lines can be found under the little finger on the right hand (or left if you are left-handed), and wrap around to the front of your hand. The longer the line, the longer the relationship or marriage.

Marriage Lines

> Short or insignificant relationships will not show up – these lines indicate long and serious romances, usually marriages.
> There may be one line representing a single serious commitment, or many lines which indicate more than one marriage or many relationships that mean a great deal to you. Small branches coming from these lines often indicate children.

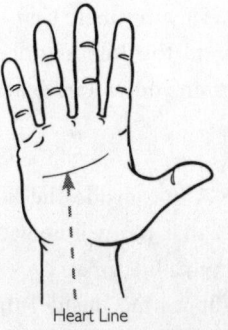

HEART LINE > A heart line that is very light represents a selfish and cold nature, while a vivid coloured heart line darker than the others tells of a passionate nature.

> A heavily chained heart line can foretell instability and emotional confusion.

> A strong heart line indicates someone confident in their sexuality and warm and generous to others.

> If the heart line dominates all other lines and stands out the most, the person is self-obsessed and may not last the distance in a serious relationship.

> A curved heart line shows a strong sex drive and a person who is a leader in their field.

> A high or low lying heart line reveals that a spiritual soulmate connection is likely.

> A straight heart line shows a warning – do not rush in to love affairs, take your time and be shrewd and smart.

> A heart line that ends in a fork is a very fortunate sign.
Note: The closer the heart line rises to the Jupiter finger (index finger), the longer the relationship you will have and the more contentment in life.

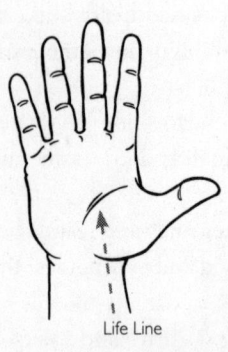

LIFE LINE > A line inside the life line indicates that you will be with a soulmate in this life time.

> Branches appearing inside the life line can also indicate births of children, depending at what age the line is found.
> Small cross bars across the life line reveal unsuccessful relationships.

Life Line

If there is a break in the line then it joins again after the break, you may reunite with a lover or family member after a split.

> A long life line doesn't literally mean a long life – it refers to your energy, vitality and staying power, and indicates that you will keep active most of your life.

- A short life line doesn't literally mean a short life, but rather an inactive one. It can also show a move to another country to live or being uprooted at an early age.
- Remember you can check the opposite hand too, to compare your original destiny with what has actually happened, and you can change what you don't like to some degree – for instance you can make your life more active and thus lengthen your life line.
- A life line that begins very high up, close to your fingers, shows that you are incredibly ambitious.
- People with life lines that start lower are not as ambitious.
- A life line that shapes like a half circle around the thumb area indicates a person who likes to stay at home and keep close to the family, who is traditional and has a love of nature.
- A very curvy life line reveals an extrovert.
- A strong life line means a person is more resilient and robust, and has stored energy to cope with life's challenges. If the life line is the strongest line on the palm you will be more inclined to pursue physical activities than intellectual pursuits and will probably excel at sports.

> A weak life line shows a lack of energy and a need to rest more.
> These people tire easily and aren't that interested in physical activity.

Note: If the life line starts strong and ends weak there could be a deterioration in your health over time, while if it starts weak and finishes strong it implies that you will change your life and improve your health later in life.

HEALTH > The type of hand you have, whether earth, air, fire or water, can give you a sign about potential health issues you need to watch out for.

EARTH HANDS > You may be susceptible to bowel and stomach problems – you need to de-stress and exercise more. Try yoga, tai chi or running, as being outdoors is also ideal. Try to avoid overindulging in the "good life" and practise moderation.

AIR HANDS > You need to relax more, as you run on nervous energy and will suffer exhaustion – you are always busy and need to say no more often! Learn to take time out and switch off with a good book, a walk in the park, swimming or anything you enjoy.

FIRE HANDS > You are running around in circles trying to please others and taking on heavy workloads, and will suffer burnout every so often. You need exercise more than the other groups and could suffer accidents from rushing around and being impulsive. It's also important not to smoke as you are susceptible to lung troubles and sore throats.

WATER HANDS > Try to avoid demanding problem people as you get so involved that you could suffer from depression due to holding on to too much baggage. Learn to let go and make time for yourself to laugh and smell the roses. Watch out for too much alcohol or drug use, as they could become dependencies.

HEALTH PROBLEMS TO LOOK FOR > A star on the heart line can indicate potential heart problems.
> Indents on the heart line mean you may suffer from migraines and tension headaches.
> An extra long head line can indicate hyperactivity and behavioural problems.
> If the head line is blurred or fuzzy this can indicate periods of mental strain.
> Lines cutting across the life line mean there may be periods of emotional upheaval and trauma.

Fingernails are also indicators of health problems.
> Speckled nails showing greyish and white shades indicate a stressful time and a possible zinc deficiency.
> Fan shaped nails reveal a tendency to run on nervous energy and being highly strung – it's a warning to rest.
> Wraparound nails, which curve around to the side of fingers, show a period of poor health, but when you're feeling better the nails will return to normal.

PALMISTRY > 203

> Horizontal ridges on nails are caused by trauma, emotional upheavals, shock or illness.
> Vertical ridges on nails are associated with stomach and intestinal problems, so have a check-up if you feel unwell.

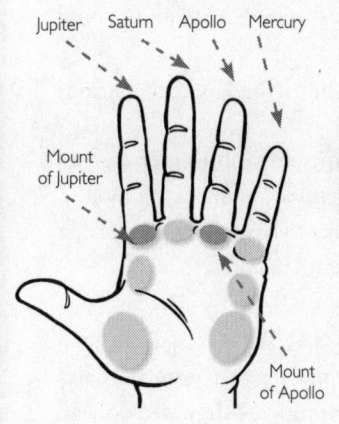

MONEY > Hands that are well padded usually indicate good financial success in life. People with these hands are prepared to work hard, whereas weak, doughy hands can indicate laziness and a desire for the good life without working for it.

> A star on the Jupiter mount is an exceptionally lucky omen.
> A star on the Apollo mount shows extraordinary skills, creative brilliance and the abilities required for fame in life.
> A star on the Apollo line represents a potential money win, and if the line continues it shows great happiness.

> A long Apollo finger is the sign of a high risk taker or gambler.
> A straight Jupiter finger shows integrity.
> The further your thumb stretches out the more aggression and power you need to reach your goals.
> A short Saturn finger reveals someone who is more cautious and sits on the fence.

EARTH HANDS > indicate someone who is prepared to work hard and will save considerable amounts of money. They are security conscious and like to have money put aside for a rainy day. They also don't like to take risks.

AIR HANDS reveal someone who is a risk taker and has good intuition when it comes to money making. They are alert and take advantage of financial opportunities – they will do well with the stock exchange and investments.

FIRE HANDS > seem to attract money more than others hands. They are adaptable to change and don't like to have all their eggs in one basket. They are creative ideas people and generally lucky. They love spending money on luxurious items and living the good life.

WATER HANDS > indicate someone who is not that interested in being wealthy. They prefer to grow spiritually rather than financially – although their creative talents will probably see them make money anyway.

TRAVEL >
EARTH HANDS > like routine, and prefer to travel to the same place each year. They are also happy to stay at home and potter around. They love the outdoors, and ideal holidays would be camping near the beach, a small hotel in a rural area or an adventure around their own country – anything that doesn't involve too much mucking around to get there or too much to pack or organise.

AIR HANDS > enjoy meeting people from all walks of life, and love romantic old cities and culture. This group of people are the most frequent travellers, and love to try different places, experience the unusual and learn about different people.

FIRE HANDS > are great risk takers and adventurers – they are like children because they love the excitement of travel and just going anywhere spontaneously. They could come home with tickets booked to travel the next day, as they are very impulsive when it comes to travel and love meeting people from other cultures.

WATER HANDS > love nature and spiritual places. Sacred sites like Egypt and Peru would be high on their travel list, as well as spiritual and health retreats, music festivals and snow fields for that wild experience of fresh open spaces and chilled air.

MOVING OMENS > Your next move of house or business is indicated with movement from the life line, a branch shooting out and up towards the Saturn mount, the padded area under the middle finger.

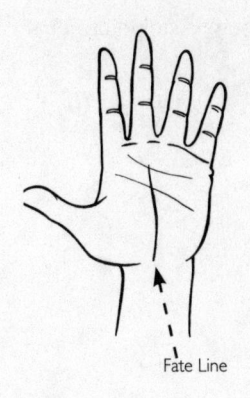

Fate Line

A break in the fate line can indicate that a person will move to another country, and branches coming from the life line moving towards the Luna mount (the padded area above your outer wrist, on the opposite side to your thumb) represent a decision between two lifestyles and being torn between which place to live and call home.

208 < PALMISTRY

Travel Lines

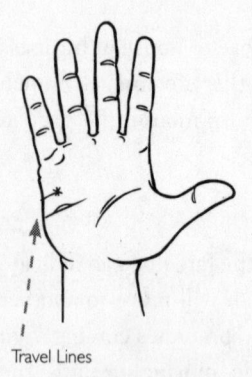

TRAVEL LINES > can also be seen at the side of the hand – the more lines there are, the more trips are indicated, and the longer they are the further away the destination.
> Stars on travel lines can predict danger, and an island on travel lines can show disappointments in the trip.

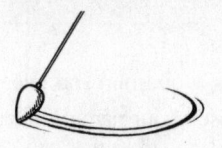

PENDULUMS > Pendulums have been used for centuries to predict anything from a person's love life, the sex of a baby, the location of a lost item to what vitamins are right for you. It is a form of dowsing, which divines the position of underground water supplies, mineral deposits, pipes, tunnels etc by the use of metal rods or a forked stick that responds to the electromagnetic frequency of the hidden object.

The use of pendulums is known as radiesthesia, and is like indoor dowsing. It uses an object hanging from a chain or something similar to divine answers. You can buy a pendulum from a new age store, in either metal, brass or crystal, or simply make your own by using a pendant on a necklace, a key on a piece of string, a wedding ring on a strand of hair, a needle on some thread or even a bead on a bit of cotton – anything like this as long as it swings easily.

To determine a yes or no answer, you must first program your pendulum to respond. Hold the chain/string/hair between the thumb and index finger of your dominant hand (the one you write with). Ask a question you know the answer to, such as: "Is my name [insert your name]?" This will establish its yes response. Then ask a question where you know the answer is no, such as: "Is my name [someone else's name]?" This will show its no response. Usually one will swing around in a circle and the other will swing backwards and forwards in a line. You can then ask it any question, and it will answer yes or no, responding to the energetic truth of the universe. To find lost objects, ask yes or no questions, such as: "Is my passport in the kitchen?" (No) "Is it in my bedroom?" (Yes) "Is it in the bedside table?" (No) "Is it in the sock drawer?" (Yes).

I have created the board opposite to give you a taste of the power of the pendulum. You can use a pendulum, holding it over the page and moving your hand gently so it hovers over each number in turn – it should swing around in a circle until it is above the number you need, where it will stop still. You can also use the board without a pendulum. Just close your eyes, spin it around three times then, with your eyes still closed, point to a spot on the page, which will have your answer. Be sure not to peek!

PENDULUMS >211

Check your answer with the meanings over the page.

1 = LOVE > This indicates fresh relationships, and that someone new and exciting is ready to come into your life.

2 = PARTNERSHIP > This can represent a new business partnership or a marriage proposal.

3 = MONEY > Opportunities will loom large in financial matters, windfalls and wealth.

4 = CAREER > Strong advancement, promotion or a new job offer is likely, and you'll be learning new skills.

5 = TRAVEL > Travel and adventure is on the horizon, so get ready!

6 = MARRIAGES/RELATIONSHIPS > Harmony and better communication is needed, but it's a favourable time for commitments and strengthening existing relationships.

7 = PROBLEMS > There are issues that must be resolved now, so face up to them, deal with them and move on.

8 = CRACKER! > This indicates an abundance of joy, happiness, good news and wealth.

9 = HEALTH > There may be health concerns for yourself or someone close to you, so get lots of rest and look after yourself.

10 = NO! > The answer to your question is no.

11 = ANGEL > You are surrounded by psychic and heavenly guidance, so open your eyes and look for the signs.

12 = SELF-IMPROVEMENT > It's time to reinvent yourself, both physically and emotionally, so invest in some new clothes or a new attitude or study a new form of healing.

13 = BEGINNINGS > A fresh start and a brand new lease of life is in the air, and there could also be a change in address.

14 = CHARITY > It's time to make a sacrifice or give of your time to someone in need.

15 = CAUTION > Be very wary at this time – all is not what it seems.

16 = ENDINGS > Get rid of all the emotional baggage, clutter and relationships that no longer serve a purpose in your life, as they are weighing you down and holding you back.

17 = FRIENDSHIPS > New friends and a lively social life await you, so join new clubs, take up a sport or hobby and enjoy this period.

18 = WISH > A wish is about to come true, so write out your affirmations now.

19 = INTUITION > You are very perceptive and intuitive at this time, and you can predict your own future through meditation.

20 = CHILDREN > This can represent a new family member through birth or marriage, or mean that your children need your advice and guidance now. A child will also make you proud.

21 = YES! > The answer to your question is yes.

PLAYING CARDS > Tarot and oracle cards have been used for centuries to divine the future, but they can be quite complicated and involved and require much practise to master. But they also evolved into the humble deck of playing cards which, surprisingly, are a great tool for predicting the future – and you can buy a pack for just a few dollars. There are different ways to use the deck. You can pull a card each morning to get a brief message for the day, or you can sit down with them and think of your question as you shuffle the deck, then pull out three cards and read them together to get an answer or guidance to the given situation. Use your intuition to see the deeper meaning of the cards and how the three messages are linked.

HEARTS >

> **Ace of hearts** = Love and happiness awaits you, ooh la la!

> **King of hearts** = A fair haired man will bring love into your life.

> **Queen of hearts** = Kind advice from a motherly figure will be very helpful to you.

> **Jack of hearts** = A great new friendship will form shortly.

> **10 of hearts** = There will be family celebrations, and a wish will come true concerning personal relationships and happy family life.

> **9 of hearts**	= An ending in a relationship will be for the better. Travel for love is also likely, and long distance communication.
> **8 of hearts**	= Unexpected surprises and gifts will come your way.
> **7 of hearts**	= There is deceit, false hopes and emotional upheavals ahead.
> **6 of hearts**	= This indicates good luck for partnerships and a spiritual soulmate.
> **5 of hearts**	= Jealous friends and backstabbers are around, be careful.
> **4 of hearts**	= Travel and long-term plans can be made regarding your personal life.

PLAYING CARDS > 219

> **3 of hearts**	=	There will be good news, with celebrations, great communication, lots of fun times and perhaps a new family member.
> **2 of hearts**	=	This indicates an engagement or proposal being put.

CLUBS >

> **Ace of clubs**	=	A cracker! Good times are here!
> **King of clubs**	=	A dark haired man will be very generous in your favour.
> **Queen of clubs**	=	A confident, dark haired businesswoman will help you.

> **Jack of clubs**	=	A young man has an offer of employment or financial opportunities for you.
> **10 of clubs**	=	This indicates business success.
> **9 of clubs**	=	You will achieve much right now.
> **8 of clubs**	=	Outstanding opportunities surround you now. Make the most of them.
> **7 of clubs**	=	Beware losses as they could occur now if care is not taken.
> **6 of clubs**	=	Patience and harmony is important right now for success in financial concerns. Don't be a doormat.
> **5 of clubs**	=	This is a turning point. Great new connections, new skills and advancement are close by.

> 4 of clubs	= Contracts, offers, long-term plans and legal issues surround you now.
> 3 of clubs	= You'll have success and be rewarded for achievements.
> 2 of clubs	= Be careful who you trust right now, as enemies loom large.

SPADES >

> Ace of spades	= Misfortune and bad luck is indicated with this card.
> King of spades	= A fair man close to you will be selfish and self serving.
> Queen of spades	= A widow or divorced woman may seek your guidance.

PLAYING CARDS

> **Jack of spades** = A young dark haired man may try to con or influence you – temptations loom large.

> **10 of spades** = This shows worry, stress and sleepless nights. Nuture yourself.

> **9 of spades** = There will be an end to a relationship or business deal.

> **8 of spades** = You will have the strength to get through a difficult period.

> **7 of spades** = Arguments, financial problems and legal disputes may occur now.

> **6 of spades** = Relationship problems need to be resolved.

> **5 of spades**	=	Happiness is nearby, you just have to move through these challenges.
> **4 of spades**	=	Ill health is indicated, so look after your wellbeing.
> **3 of spades**	=	Heartache, loss and separation from a loved one is revealed.
> **2 of spades**	=	You're at a crossroads – a major decision must be made now.

DIAMONDS >

> **Ace of diamonds**	=	There is massive change, rebirth and reinvention around you. This could also indicate a birth.

> King of diamonds	=	A fair haired man will make you an offer in your favour.
> Queen of diamonds	=	Avoid a gossipy woman who is irritating and annoying.
> Jack of diamonds	=	An unreliable friend or business associate is jealous of you.
> 10 of diamonds	=	There are outstanding opportunities for moving closer to your goals.
> 9 of diamonds	=	An end will bring on a new beginning – let go of the past as this is a time of enormous growth.
> 8 of diamonds	=	Wealth and major purchases are indicated.

> 7 of diamonds	=	Arguments and financial worries may affect you now.
> 6 of diamonds	=	Don't let a relationship problem affect you – work through it.
> 5 of diamonds	=	This is a turning point and a time of change and new directions.
> 4 of diamonds	=	You can lay foundations for the rest of the year now. There are very prosperous times ahead.
> 3 of diamonds	=	Legal issues are indicated, with contracts being offered and rewards for past efforts.
> 2 of diamonds	=	Balance in personal and business relationships is needed.

PSYCHIC ANIMALS > This animal oracle is a fun way to divine your future and receive guidance. Using a pin or just your finger, close your eyes, ask your question then feel yourself being guided to pinpointing one of the animals, which will reveal its wisdom to you. Open your eyes, look at the one you picked and read its meaning over the page. You can also use a pendulum – hold it over the page and gently move it around – it will suddenly stop swinging over the animal you need guidance from. These animals may also come to you in dreams to share their messages with you.

PSYCHIC ANIMALS > 227

Ape	Horse	Bull	Tiger
Dog	Rabbit	Bird	Cat
Swan	Wolf	Eagle	Snake
Boar	Raven	Owl	Bee

Ape >	Great fun is in store, and socially you'll be having the time of your life. Relax and enjoy it, and know that you deserve it.
Bee >	A very hectic and busy time awaits you – you'll be a busy bee! – but money gains are likely as a result, and all your efforts will pay off.
Bird >	This indicates that travel may be close by, or a change of residence or job could be in the wind. Either way, you'll be spreading your wings and flying.
Boar >	This indicates victory and triumph, so enjoy the rewards of your hard work. You're a winner!
Bull >	Do not be a doormat – stand up for your rights and get your feelings out in the open.

PSYCHIC ANIMALS > 229

> The bull has strength and purpose, and you need to channel this sense of self to get through the obstacles that are facing you.

Cat >	You're on a spiritual journey. Your intuition is extremely strong right now, and you will receive messages to guide you. Place a picture of a cat in a purple envelope and keep it in your wallet or bag for seven days to assist you.
Dog >	Your friends will be loyal right now, and will help you through a troubled time. Accept their help and support – that's what friends are for.
Eagle >	This is the ultimate animal for a shining destiny. A cracker of a time awaits you, with success professionally and personally and a golden period of super bliss.

Horse >	You'll soon be galloping to splendid victories. Write your wish on a piece of gold paper and fold it up with a picture or a drawing of a horse.
Owl >	Wisdom and sound advice will be forthcoming, so pay attention to signs and messages that come from unlikely places.
Rabbit >	This could indicate a pregnancy or the planning of a new project close to your heart. It's also a very passionate time, but be careful of deceit.
Raven >	This reveals that you have protection from above, with spiritual guidance from angels or deceased loved ones. Burn a white candle nightly and visualise the raven. Ask it questions and see if you can discern its answers.

Snake >	Although they symbolise wisdom, choosing the snake could indicate losses in your life or that someone you know is a backstabber. If this is true get that person out of your life.
Swan >	You will be infused with the beauty and grace of a swan. Romance is electric, and singles will soon meet someone outstanding.
Tiger >	This regal cat indicates promotion on the work front, great career moves or success in learning new hobbies or skills. It's a time of self-improvement and success.
Wolf >	Danger and deceit surrounds you now, and you have the potential to be taken in by it. Be on your guard.

ANIMAL OMENS

Bees > Bees entering your home mean good luck, while bees landing on your head indicate that you'll get a promotion or achieve career success.

Birds > Birds flying into your home mean there is an important message trying to be conveyed to you. A willy wagtail close to your door or inside means someone is watching over you, and you're receiving angelic guidance or messages from deceased loved ones.

Bird poop > If it lands on your head, money is arriving. If it lands on your left side, someone from the past will return. If it lands on the right side, a new and valuable friendship will begin. And if it lands on your car, a lucky time is in store for the next six months.

Butterflies >	If a pretty butterfly flies into the house it is an omen of good luck. If a white butterfly is the first one you see, you'll have a great year ahead. If there are three together however, there are tough and challenging times ahead.
Cats >	Ask a cat a question. If the right paw moves forward first then the answer is yes; if the left paw moves first then the answer is no. If you dream of a white cat it indicates wealth.
Dogs >	If a strange dog follows you, trouble is in store so beware.
Dove >	To see a dove indicates that love will be sizzling in the near future.
Ducks >	If you hear a duck quacking eight times it foretells prosperity.

Eagle > Make a wish, because seeing an eagle, especially in flight, is the best omen ever.

Ferret > If you encounter a ferret it means you will find success within two weeks.

Lizard > Seeing a lizard in an unusual place indicates that bad news is coming.

Magpie > Two or more is lucky, but one on its own is thought to be bad luck.

Spiders > A spider on your clothes means good fortune awaits you. A spider running down its web reveals travel. If you run into a spider web visitors will be arriving soon. And a spider seen in the morning can indicate a bad day ahead.

IS YOUR PET PSYCHIC? > Many studies and anecdotal evidence have revealed that animals are psychic, and also that they can form strong intuitive and psychic bonds with their owners. Many dogs will know just before their diabetic owner's blood sugar levels start to drop, and try to warn them. There are also countless stories of animals who have found their way back to their owners after being lost or moving house, even across cities and states.

Test your ESP connection with your pet and their psychic ability. Maybe you can get a telepathic message to them!

DOGS >

Wait until your dog is sleeping. Make sure your friend or partner watches them. Go upstairs or into a different room, taking the dog's lead with you (don't let the dog see you take it though). Now meditate or visualise taking your dog for a walk – the people you see, the parks your pet runs in, the flowers and trees you go past, the smell of other dogs he meets, your dog's enjoyment of it all – imagine and visualise it all. Now think: "Walkies!" Say the word in your mind. A few minutes into your ESP testing, your friend should wake the dog – which will probably run straight up the stairs or to the room you're in ready for his walk, or start barking to go outside, all prepared and anxious for his walk.

CATS >

Wait until your cat is resting and relaxing or sleeping. Have your friend or accomplice watch her carefully. Go upstairs or into a far away room and visualise her favourite fish or chicken dinner. Picture the smell, the cat eating the scrumptious dinner and purring. Take it all in for a few minutes, then think the word: "Dinner!" Say it a few times to yourself in your head. After a few minutes have your accomplice wake the cat, and watch her either run to where you are, licking her lips, race over to her food bowl or start purring around your friend's legs ready for dinner.

RUNES > Runes have been used for thousands of years for writing, divination and even magic. They are a set of symbols derived from an alphabet of Germanic origin, and were used and worn for protection, healing and to predict the future. They work best when you have a specific question, and they can give you a great deal of guidance along your path. You can make your own set with small stones or pieces of wood – simply draw the symbol on each one, then keep them in a cloth sack and pull one out when you are in need of guidance. Alternatively just close your eyes, turn this book around three times and circle the page with your finger, eyes still shut, until you feel drawn to a part of the page. Point to one of the symbols then open your eyes and look up the meaning of your chosen rune.

238 < RUNES

Rune	Name
M	Ehwaz
H	Hagalaz
B	Berkano
P	Wunjo
↑	Nauthiz
◊	Othala
R	Raidho
↑	Tiwaz
L	Laguz
J	Eihwaz
I	Isa
Y	Algiz
S	Jera
◊	Ingwaz
F	Ansuz
S	Sowilo
X	Gebo
F	Fehu
Þ	Thurisaz
M	Mannaz
Γ	Perthro
<	Kenaz
⋈	Dagaz
∩	Uruz

RUNES

Fehu >	Ambitions satisfied, wealth, love conquered, rewards.
Uruz >	Changes, endings and new beginnings, staying positive and persistent, courage needed to make decisions, vitality.
Thurisaz >	New options and opportunities, reviewing your past and letting go of what is not necessary in your future.
Ansuz >	Gaining knowledge, messages from above, secrets revealed, expect the unexpected, new relationships, new business connections arriving.
Raidho >	Taking control of your life, travel, movement, self-healing, reunions, possible change of address.

Kenaz >	Learning new skills, solving problems, conclusions, intense emotions and passion, breakthrough in troublesome relationships.
Gebo >	Partnerships, marriages, unions, commitments, fortune smiles, positive blast of energy, new-found hope and great joy.
Wunjo >	Tremendous fulfilment, turning point, better way of living and sense of wellbeing.
Hagalaz >	Disruption, chaos, emotional upheavals, negative events, a wake-up call.
Nauthiz >	Pain, confinement, restricting circumstances, delays, disappointments – review your plans now.

Isa >	Activities frozen, letting go of the past and closing necessary doors, realising a stalemate has been reached.
Jera >	Fertility, reaping what you have sown, rewards coming thick and fast for past efforts.
Eihwaz >	Protection. Be ready to stand up for yourself. Think before you act, face up to your challenges. Be assertive and bold. Take a risk.
Perthro >	Great wisdom, powerful forces of change, a sudden unexpected new relationship or business connections.
Algiz >	Protection from pain, don't sweep problems under the carpet, learn from your mistakes and past experiences, beware who you get involved with or trust.

Sowilo >	Perfection, bliss, great power, achieving goals.
Tiwaz >	Victory, a win.
Berkano >	Renewal, a birth, fresh new beginnings and opportunities, reinventing yourself, a makeover.
Ehwaz >	Movement, overcoming obstacles, challenges, time of transition.
Mannaz >	Giving selflessly, making sacrifices, charitable work.
Laguz >	Motherhood, great satisfaction with emotional needs, personal fulfilment.
Ingwaz >	Birth, fertility, marriage, happy harmonious existing relationships. New life, new partner, great communication and creativity.

Dagaz >	A new optimistic attitude sees magnificent progress, important personal breakthroughs, prosperity.
Othala >	Beneficial gain, a chance to learn new skills, possible inheritance or money opportunity.

SCRYING > This method is divination by seeing images and visions reflected in a surface, whether it be a crystal ball, a dark mirror, a bowl of water, a black crystal, a lake or something else. It has been used throughout many cultures since ancient times.

Crystallomancy, or gazing into a crystal ball, is an ancient form of scrying, made popular in movies about gypsies and fortune tellers.

Catoptromancy involves looking into a mirror to see images, although often these mirrors are made of polished bronze, metal or stone rather than glass.

The great seer Nostradamus, whose prophecies are still drawing attention five centuries later, used water scrying and mirror gazing to predict many major events. This is similar to crystal ball gazing, although you use the surface of a mirror or a bowl of water to see the images in. Use a large deep bowl made of glass, silver or brass, and place it on a tripod if possible. Ink can also be added to the water if you prefer, as this may make it easier for you to see the visions. Do this at night. Peer into the surface of the water. Large ripples will begin to appear, and you may even get images. Try doing this on the full moon outside under the stars or on the balcony.

Scrying takes a long time to master, so be patient and practise a lot. Keep a journal of what you see and use your intuition to discover the meaning of your visions.

CRYSTAL BALL GAZING > First find your crystal ball. You can buy them at new age stores and crystal shops, or quite cheaply at a market. Any kind is fine, as long as it is round or oval and free of bubbles.

First create the right relaxed atmosphere. Dress in comfortable loose clothes, and light a candle, preferably white or purple. Now let the energy flow and start gazing at the ball. Don't try to make sense of anything, just relax and stare and feel a sort of tingle throughout your body. You should start to see clouds appear.

> If the clouds are moving upwards this is very positive.

> If they are moving downwards they are negative to you or the person you are reading for.

> White clouds are very good to see and represent good times ahead.

> If you see a little bright spot through the cloud shapes, like the sun trying to break through, you can expect a great improvement in your finances or health.

- If there is a dull light trying to break through and separate the clouds, this is a warning to get some rest or check out your health.

- Green clouds represent good health, vitality, the positive flow of energy and wealth opportunities.

- Blue clouds represent times of peace, safety and harmony.

- Pink clouds represent love and family happiness.

- Gold or silver clouds are the ultimate indication of wealth, love and new life energies – they're wonderful colours to see.

- Violet clouds indicate an increase in spirituality, messages from a deceased loved one or taking a new spiritual path.

- Red, yellow and orange clouds indicate that you must be aware – these are warning colours in crystal balls or mirrors.

You may even see images in the ball – use your intuition to divine their meaning, for instance a red car indicates danger, while a green car indicates a prosperous journey, fresh starts or even a new car. Also consult the cloud shapes in the air reading section for possible meanings.

The more you practise the better you will become, so don't expect too much straight away. It took me ages to master this. Make sure you are feeling relaxed, as it's almost impossible to be psychic when you are stressed or upset. Try some deep breathing to relax before you start.

TABLETS OF FATE > Tablets of Fate were sold by fortune tellers in the 17th century, but were used long before then as well. They were made up of a square shaped piece of paper with 16 numbers on it – you close your eyes, spin the paper and point to a spot on it. Whichever number you land on reveals the answer to your question. The numbers correspond to the vibrations of specific planets and their responsibilities.

> Questions about love are answered by the **Tablet of Venus**.

> Questions about business, work and money are answered by the **Tablet of Mars**.

> Questions about worries, legal issues and justice are answered by the **Tablet of Jupiter**.

> Questions about your home life, relatives and friends are answered by the **Tablet of the Rising Moon**.

> Questions of timing in relation to love, career and travel, or anything you are concerned about, are answered by the **Tablet of the Rising Sun**.

You can make your own Tablets of Fate and read your own fortune. Just check out the details that follow for each specific one.

```
5    11    1    9

14    7    4    12

8    3    16    2

6    15    10    13
```

TABLET OF VENUS > To answer a question relating to love, you need to create a Tablet of Venus. Simply copy the numbers above on to a square piece of cardboard or thick paper, keeping them in the same order and ensuring they are all evenly spaced. Next close your eyes and spin the paper around three times with your fingers. Ask your question aloud, then with your eyes still closed, use a pencil or your finger to land on a number. See the following meanings for the answer to your relationship question.

> 1 = A soulmate connection is close by.

> 2 = You have emotional upheavals to deal with around all personal relationships.

> 3 = News of a wedding or birth is likely, and a commitment may also be made.

> 4 = Quarrels, arguments or separations are indicated.

> 5 = Everything is progressing in your favour, so stay positive.

> 6 = Love is sizzling – you're about to meet someone new and exciting. This can also indicate the birth of a child.

> 7 = There is baggage and secrets around a relationship, so good communication is needed.

> 8 = Your marriage potential is high, good news awaits.

> 9 = Long distance communication is lucky for love right now, and travel is shown.

> 10 = You have a secret admirer.

> 11 = You will dream about your partner, or if single your next lover.

> 12 = Social fun and meeting great new people is indicated. Pop the champagne, as a celebration is also close.

> 13 = Think before you act – don't be too impulsive! Tread lightly at this time.

> 14 = Passion is oozing right now, so put the "do not disturb" sign on the bedroom door!

> 15 = A chance meeting incites feelings you have not felt for a long time.

> 16 = Starting a new course, exercise program or hobby will lead to a new love if you are single.

8	13	6	2
3	5	4	12
10	7	9	16
14	1	15	11

TABLET OF MARS > This tablet can be used for divination and predicting answers to questions about business, work and money. Simply copy the numbers above on to a square piece of cardboard or thick paper, keeping them in the same order and ensuring they are all evenly spaced. Then close your eyes, spin it around eight times as you think of your question, then circle the page with your finger or a pin. Stop when you feel the vibe and point to a number. Open your eyes and see what number you have selected, and find its meaning, and the answer to your question in the following chart.

> 1 = Fresh opportunities surround the near future. This is a time to be bold, daring and assertive, not to sit on the fence.

> 2 = Be patient now and don't rush into any money decisions. Reorganise your budget.

> 3 = Long distance communication will bring good luck and opportunity presently.

> 4 = Now is the time to make long-term plans. Lots of extra effort is needed though.

> 5 = A change in job, expansion in business, money ideas and gains are likely – but don't be too impulsive over the coming months.

> 6 = You will make dynamic connections and be popular on the work front, with good luck in new ventures in the next two weeks.

> 7	=	There are obstacles and challenges around all money and career matters at this time. You will learn new skills in the near future and specialise in new areas of your career.
> 8	=	You will celebrate achievements and have splendid successes in all undertakings. A win is also indicated.
> 9	=	Be careful of deception and deceit now and beware who you trust. Don't lend money or tell your ideas to anyone.
> 10	=	Travel will provide you with new connections and opportunities. Goals will be reached and you'll be rewarded for past efforts.
> 11	=	Your intuition is so strong now – pay particular attention to dreams and gut feelings regarding your business and financial concerns.

> 12 = You are communicating brilliantly and will have luck in financial undertakings. Put your plans into action.

> 13 = Don't spend money at present, as unexpected bills are about to surface.

> 14 = It's an excellent time to sell anything. Have a garage sale, clear away clutter and give to charity. Sacrifices made at this time will increase your success.

> 15 = Business or financial meetings will prove fruitful now and help you make more money over the next 12 months than you ever thought possible. Place a jade plant at your front door.

> 16 = This indicates losses, endings, turmoil and things not working out as planned. Hang in there though – a turning point for the financially better is unfolding.

```
        5
     2    11
   10   1    36
  4   8   3    14
   15   16   12
     9    7
        1
```

TABLET OF JUPITER > This tablet is to do with questions of doubt, worries, legal issues and justice. Simply copy the numbers above on to a square piece of cardboard or thick paper, keeping them in the same order and ensuring they are all evenly spaced. Then light a gold candle, take three deep breaths, and when totally relaxed close your eyes and spin the paper around a few times as you think of your question. Using your finger or a pin, prick the Tablet then open your eyes and see which number you landed on. The meanings that follow will give you the answer to your question.

> 1 = By standing up for yourself and getting everything out in the open you will feel much better. Write out all your problems on a piece of paper then pass them through the candle flame to destroy them.

> 2 = A friend will give you helpful advice soon, so pay attention to what they say and try to see its value.

> 3 = A win is likely. Wear red as much as you can or write out a wish and place it inside a red envelope.

> 4 = Justice will be served within six months.

> 5 = After all the turmoil of recent times, a better way of living will open up and the sun will shine again.

> 6 = An ending will bring a new beginning – the key words are: "Let go of the past."

> 7 = Your strength is being put to the test, but you will be able to move mountains, so stay strong and focused.

> 8 = Avoid jealous and negative people, as they are stopping you from reaching your goals and being happy.

> 9 = Long-term decisions need to be made this week regarding your current worries and questions.

> 10 = There will be a conclusion to a long drawn out situation, worry or legal issue.

> 11 = A time of anxiety will end, with a happier period of life about to begin. Place yellow flowers inside your home.

> 12 = Communication is the key now. Place a rose quartz crystal in your bag or wallet.

> 13 = There is some deceit or corruption around you, so be aware.

> 14 = Reality is not as bad as your fears and doubts would have you believe – help is on the way.

> 15 = You will start to journey away from a difficult period from now on.

> 16 = Stop being used and treated as a doormat – it's time to stick up for yourself and get back your self-esteem.

TABLETS OF FATE > 263

```
        10
     2     16
  6           4
13             7
 8             9
 1            15
  14         11
    12   5  3
```

TABLET OF THE RISING MOON > This tablet is used to answer questions concerning your home life, relatives and friends. This can only be used on the night of a new moon. First, create the Tablet, which is comprised of a circle with the numbers from 1-16 arranged in a circle in the same order as above. Next, close your eyes and turn the Tablet around three times while thinking of your question, then point to a number or use a pin to land on one. Open your eyes and see which number you chose. Check its meaning in the table that follows to find the answer to your question.

> 1 = A new address is a possibility, or you may acquire a new family member through marriage or birth.

> 2 = Health is a concern right now around a family member or close friend. Place a picture of them in a green frame.

> 3 = A wish for yourself or a family member will come true within six months. Write out your wish and place it in a gold envelope under your bed.

> 4 = You will be disappointed by a friend or relative's attitude. Wear pink as much as you can or keep a rose quartz crystal close by to protect yourself from negativity.

> 5 = Arguments around your home are indicated – be careful of using heated words you will regret! Get rid of all clutter in the home and have a big bowl of fresh fruit and a vase of fresh flowers.

> 6 = Harmony and good news will be cause for a big celebration, and if you are single a friend may introduce you to a sexy new lover.

> 7 = Obstacles and problems to be solved are indicated. Take your shoes off when entering your home to leave these problems outside.

> 8 = Stop worrying so much – the finances around your family are improving! Place nine gold painted nuggets glued together in your front garden.

> 9 = Family reunions are approaching – be sure to plant some colourful flowers near your front door or have some inside in a vase, and play bright happy music.

> 10 = An in-law may act as a troublemaker and backstabber at this time, so be aware but forgiving.

> 11 = Dreams of a deceased friend or close family member are likely from now on. Light a white candle whenever you need a message from them.

> 12 = Champagne and celebrations over a family reward or win are likely. Place three Chinese coins on your key ring.

> 13 = Are you at your healthiest? Do you need to exercise more or have a check-up? Place a picture of yourself in a green photo frame.

> 14 = A younger family member has many secret worries around school or their job. Put a citrine crystal in their bedroom and a small dragon facing the front door in your home.

> 15 = A relative or close friend will tell you a secret that will completely change the way you think and feel about a certain someone.

> 16 = Separation and tears are indicated for yourself, a family member or close friend. Display a sundial or pictures of the sun in your home or garden.

268 < TABLETS OF FATE

10	3	6	13
8	15	1	5
9	11	7	16
2	14	12	4

TABLET OF THE RISING SUN > This tablet is used to determine the timing of events or issues regarding love, career and travel, or anything else you are concerned about. It will give you a time frame for your query. Simply create a Tablet on a piece of cardboard or heavy paper with the numbers arranged in the pattern above, making sure they are spaced evenly apart. Next close your eyes and speak your question out loud. With your eyes still closed, turn the card around then stick a pin or use your finger to land on a number. Read the meaning that follows to discover when and how your problem or question will progress.

> 1 = It will happen within six months – but stay strong and focused and stop changing your mind!

> 2 = You are wasting your time – there is no hope at all, so stop fooling yourself.

> 3 = It could happen within two weeks if you stay positive. You can make this happen by your own means.

> 4 = Never – forget it!

> 5 = Before next year if you start communicating what you really want and making plans now.

> 6 = You need to make many changes first and learn to communicate better and stop bottling things up inside.

> 7 = It's unlikely to happen at all. Deception seems to be around you at present, so make sure you know who you can trust.

> 8 = The outcome will be better than you think – although there are a few challenges and hurdles to get through first.

> 9 = It will happen as soon as you close the necessary doors and get rid of all the baggage that is blocking your progress.

> 10 = It will occur within three weeks.

> 11 = It will happen after you put in the effort, change your attitude and get rid of those users in your life.

> 12 = You know you have to make a decision before it will happen, but positive vibes surround you.

> 13 = It will take place within the next year.

> 14 = What you hope for will occur soon – but lots of effort is required now to ensure it does.

> 15 = Only time will tell. Hang in there and have patience. Lots will manifest in your favour and wishes around personal relationships will come true.

> 16 = Sooner than you think – after you reassess your priorities and decide what you really do want to do.

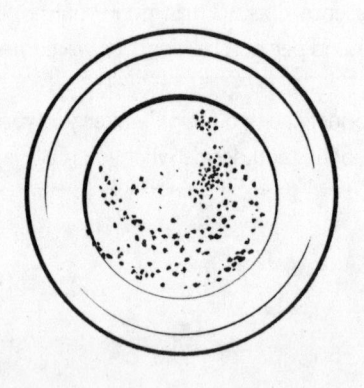

TEA LEAF READING > Tasseography, or the reading of tea leaves, is an ancient form of divination practised by the Chinese as well as the gypsies and many other cultures. It interprets the shapes of the tea leaves left at the bottom of the cup after you've had a cup of tea. It can also be performed with the granules left from coffee or the sediment left at the bottom of a glass of red wine.

DRINK TO DIVINE > To do a tea leaf reading, make sure not to leave sugar at the bottom of your cup or you'll be unlucky in love. Stir well before drinking. If bubbles appear in your brew, this indicates that you are going to be lucky. Swoop them out with your teaspoon and make a wish while drinking them. If there are leaves floating on top you will receive a message within three days.

When brewing a pot, use nice thick leaf tea. Sip your drink slowly while thinking of a question. Leave a teaspoon of tea in the bottom of the cup. Holding the cup in your left hand, move it in a circle three times, concentrating on your question, then tip the liquid out on to the saucer, leaving the tea leaves in the bottom of the cup. Check out the shapes they have made and look at the following list of meanings to see your future.

LUCKY OMENS >
Angel >   Good news is coming, especially in love.

Animals >	A great omen – you'll make new friends and have luck and good finances.
Apple >	Major achievements are indicated.
Arch >	Overseas travel will occur.
Baby >	Near the handle this represents a birth. It can also mean new ventures.
Balloon >	Adventure and successful opportunities.
Bells >	Expect good news.
Bird >	A sign of good fortune and prosperity, especially if wings are extended.
Boat >	If it's heading away from the handle it indicates reunions, heading towards the handle you'll be receiving visitors.

Book >	You'll be learning new skills.
Bouquet >	A lucky sign that can mean marriage or a proposal of some kind.
Broom >	Changes are ahead.
Cat >	Great new friends are coming – but if it's jumping there could be jealousy.
Circle >	Marriage or a relationship – but if it's broken, a relationship will be too.
Elephant >	Good health.
Face >	You'll make new friendships.
Fish >	Abundance and wealthy times.

TEA LEAF READING

Horse >	Excellent for singles, this indicates a soulmate or fabulous new lover.
Ladder >	Work hard and you will get to the top.
Spider >	Indicates great news and healthy finances.
Star >	Make a wish – it will come true!

BAD OMENS >

Bat >	Danger.
Bear >	Move cautiously or you could lose everything.
Chain >	Don't have your eggs in so many baskets.
Coffin >	Death or the end of something.
Harp >	Don't be so trusting.

Mountains >	Obstacles and challenges are indicated.
Parrot >	Be careful who you talk to about your plans.
Snake >	Be wary of being ripped off.
Weapons >	Knives, hammers, axe or arrows etc indicate danger and deceit.

COFFEE CUP READING > Like tea leaf readings, these are done with a cup as though you are reading a crystal ball. It is best to use Turkish or Greek coffee, which leave a lot of residue after the coffee has been consumed. The patterns left from the residue inside the cup will trigger psychic insight. Make sure the person you are reading for is in a relaxed state and takes their time to drink the coffee. If it is rushed you will not be able to read the cup accurately.

OMENS

Angel >	You have guidance and support from higher places. Spiritual growth is indicated.
Ant >	Plans will come to fruition and hard work will bring home the bacon.
Baby >	A birth, or the beginning of a new project.
Bear >	Decisions will have to be made.
Bee >	New friendships, reunions and celebrations.
Bells >	Surprising news is ahead – the closer to the brim the better and if it's right down the bottom it may be bad news.
Candle >	Your intuition is strong.

Circle >	Marriage or births, but if the ring is broken it could indicate a separation.
Dog >	You have loyal friends.
Door >	A fresh opportunity.
Horse >	Victory, power and strength.
Line >	A straight line indicates a trouble free period, the longer the line, the better it is. A bumpy line reveals challenges ahead.
Man/woman >	A visitor is approaching, in your favour. Could indicate romance for singles.
Numbers >	These indicate the time periods of an upcoming change.
Owl >	Wisdom and good advice are coming to you.

Plane >	Travel.
Star >	A wish will come true.
Tree >	You'll make new friends. A palm tree means a holiday.
Weapons >	You are cautioned about danger and enemies.

the fortune teller

ABOUT THE AUTHOR > Sharina is a highly accurate psychic whose gift is foreseeing the future with the use of numbers, voice, body language and strong feelings – primarily a strong sense of knowing. She had her first otherworldy experience when she was six years old, when she would see things about people before they happened. When she was 10 she had a near death experience where she saw a golden light that seemed to stretch all over the room in the shape of a person – and was given the message that she would be okay. *"I was sure this was God, but no one believed me."*

Sharina started making predictions that would come true, from exactly when an event would happen to what it would be, things such as marriages, divorces, children, world wars, sports events, real estate booms and election results. People began to take her talents seriously.

She started her radio career in 1990 on Stan Zemanek's program on 2UE, and was an instant hit. Following this success the station launched her own show, Sharina's Psychic Encounters, which she still hosts today.

She has an astrology column in the *Sun Weekly,* which is syndicated across Australia, and has appeared in *New Idea* and *Woman's Day.* She has also appeared on many TV shows, including "Good Morning Australia", "Midday", "Beauty and the Beast" and "A Current Affair".

She is currently involved with her own live on the web TV show, teaching the psychic arts in a fun way, and performs sell-out club shows around Australia. Visit: www.sharina.com.au or Email: sharina@bigpond.net.au

> NOTES <

> NOTES <

> NOTES <

> NOTES <

> NOTES <

> NOTES <

HAY HOUSE TITLES OF RELATED INTEREST >

BOOKS >

Adventures of a Psychic, *by Sylvia Browne*

A Stream of Dreams, *by Leon Nacson*

Born Knowing, *by John Holland*

Chakra Clearing, *by Doreen Virtue, Ph.D.*

Conversations with the Other Side, *by Sylvia Browne*

Diary of a Psychic, *by Sonia Choquette*

CARD DECKS >

Archangel Oracle Cards, *by Doreen Virtue, Ph.D.*

Healing with the Angels Oracle Cards, *by Doreen Virtue, Ph.D.*

The Oracle Tarot, *by Lucy Cavendish*

Heart and Soul, *by Sylvia Browne*

Messages from your Angels Oracle Cards,
by Doreen Virtue, Ph.D.

We hope you enjoyed this Hay House book.
If you'd like to receive a free catalogue featuring additional
Hay House books and products, or if you'd like information
about the Hay Foundation, please contact:

Hay House Australia Pty. Ltd.
18/36 Ralph St., Alexandria NSW 2015
Phone: 612-9669-4299 • *Fax:* 612-9669-4144
www.hayhouse.com.au

Published and distributed in the USA by:
Hay House, Inc. • P.O. Box 5100 • Carlsbad, CA 92018-5100
www.hayhouse.com® • www.hayfoundation.org
Phone: (760) 431-7695 • *Fax:* (760) 431-6948

Published and distributed in the United Kingdom by:
Hay House UK, Ltd. • 292 Kensal Road, London W10 5BE
Phone: (020) 8962 1230 • *Fax:* (020) 8962 1239
www.hayhouse.co.uk • info@hayhouse.co.uk

Published and distributed in the Republic of South Africa by:
Hay House SA (Pty), Ltd., P.O. Box 990, Witkoppen 2068
• *Phone/Fax:* 27-11-706-6612 • orders@psdprom.co.za